Got Me Ready

From Victim to Victor

ARTIE LEE NOLEN

Unless otherwise noted, Scripture quotations are from the New King James Version of the Bible. Copyright 1979, 1980, 1982 by Thomas Nelson, Inc. Publishers.

Phoenix Publishing House, LLC

Publishers since 2016

P. O. BOX 154855

Lufkin, TX 75904

(844) 974-8300

www.phoenixpubllc.com

Printed in the United States of America

ISBN: 978-1-955235-11-2

DEDICATION

I sympathetically dedicate this book to all survivors of this one man's horror; through our different traumatic experiences, we have formed a behind-the-scenes blended family of past offenses. I know firsthand the strength and endurance required to keep waking up, keeping your head up while feeling so low to the ground. Some of us may never cross paths but know your suffering is worth being heard, acknowledged, and is essential to your fulfillment.

"Each child belongs to all of us and they will bring us a tomorrow in direct relation to the responsibility we have shown them."

Maya Angelou

DISCLAIMER

This book is a memoir. It reflects the author's present recollections of experiences over time. Some names and characteristics have been changed, some events have been compressed, and some dialogue has been recreated.

CONTENT TRIGGER WARNING

This book includes a victim's recount of horrendous acts of sexual assault, domestic violence, stalking, and physical violence. We acknowledge that this content may be difficult.

We also encourage you to care for your safety and well-being.

TABLE OF CONTANTS

PREFACE

This memoir exposes the traumatic years I endured as a small girl. At the age of five, my mother met and quickly married one of Texas's most violent serial pedophiles Mr. Melvin Henry Crosby, Sr. (*Emphasis on Sr.*). This will be the only time you see his name in this book. As we advance, pronouns he/him and other unsavory words will refer to him. He is now a seventy-five-year-old, skilled predominantly in brutality and pedophilia. I hope to validate my pain and encourage self-love and well-being to all survivors and their mothers who have endured tremendous agony. Unfortunately, they were blindsided by hidden intentions. I pray they also will find a platform to heal by speaking up and speaking out.

Memoir is a pleasant-sounding sophisticated word that sounds like men/war. A play on words but quite ironic. The warriors in place to protect me as a child directly or indirectly battled against me. As a small girl, I had to fight grown men for my rightful place in society. My mama's new husband was the first to conquer. I am a conqueror, and I want the world to know it's a possibility.

The thought of him being free once again to destroy another child's innocence keeps me up at night. The only time he was not molesting children was when he was incarcerated. Mr. Crosby Sr.'s rap sheet is extensive. It is a memoir of sorts, a history book of his offenses. A very challenging read for most tender eyes. Atrocious behaviors toward children, I respectfully will not share. Nonetheless, his criminal record is available for purchase online if your curiosity takes you there.

Please share my prayer that God binds his hands so that he never touches another child. Regardless of his desires, the reality is there are millions of sexual predators to replace him on any given day. There are millions of children being hurt daily by them. Regardless of the time he spent locked away, it can never pay for the brutal realities suffered or generations of connections severed by his cruel hands.

Pedophiles very methodically seek and destroy any sense of safety in children and are very grateful to render them useless and incapable of experiencing true love. I intend to prove that the Devil is a liar. I am whole, and I am an essential child of God. No weapon formed against me has prospered! SOMEDAY PEOPLE WILL FORM A REVOLUTION AGAINST PEDOPHILIA... until then, we must remain aware and proactive for all children's well-being.

ACKNOWLEDGMENT

I must express to the fullest my gratitude to a special aunt, Samantha "Mack" Nolen, for opening up her heart and home to me when I needed her the most. Though she is no longer amongst the living, her influence on me will never die. Mack was the first to express her love to me and the first to encourage my sense of power and relevance. She would say, "Don't let nobody run over you. The bigger they are, the harder they fall." She gave me a "kick-ass and take names" mentality. In her forty-seven short years on earth, she made quite an impact on many lives, spreading love with an iron fist.

CHAPTER 1

REVELATION

According to Wikipedia, Bullard, Texas, had a population of about three hundred in 1960. Enda and Hewsville were the town's earlier names. It was later renamed after a confederate soldier John H. Bullard. Hewsville has such a Cat in The Hat ring to it; it would have fit perfectly in my childhood horror story. Bullard is adorned with trees from every species. Almost everyone had the typical fruit trees: pecan, peach, pear, persimmon, and plum. When in season, fruit was a staple. Unfortunately, the winter months were not as gracious. Bullard, better known by my family as "the pinery" possibly because of the walls of trees lining dirt roads. Funny thing, I don't recall seeing many pine trees.

Bullard can be a deafening quiet country town. Most of the farms were either cattle raisers or crop producers. Barbed wire was fastened to tree branch posts that adorned juicy wild berries for the taking. To this day, those wild berries still line the fences and are as sweet and juicy as they ever were. Despite the time that has lapsed, my anxiety level rises immediately when I stand on that land. I finally realized I had repeatedly been returning to the initial crime scene—the place where betrayal, deceit, falsehood, fraud, hypocrisy, and disinformation originated. Therefore, I must consider my road trip destination more carefully going forward.

On the grandest night to date, December 14, 1960, the most beautiful milk chocolate baby girl arrived into the waiting arms of proud parents, Bobby and Josephine Jessie. They were sweethearts since high school—what a lovely young family. The baby's room is breathtaking and adorned with everything a new baby needs. First, both sides of the family gathered around welcoming a new life. Then, they gathered in the living room, whispering prayers and praising God.

That's the scenario we deserved, so I made it up. Playing pretend is child's play. It has its place in early development, but it's time to put that away as an adult. Pretending to love someone is one of the cruelest of deceptions because the recipient's emotional wellbeing is deliberately disregarded and treated like a toy that you've gotten tired of playing with. That kind of lie can totally destroy a person's self-esteem, especially if that person is fragile to begin with. Mama was that person that was totally disregarded. There is no way in hell my father loved her or me.

Bobby had proudly walked away. That single act of neglecting his parental responsibilities impacted our lives more than he ever cared to consider. Mama and Bobby had both attended Stanton High School. I assume that is where they met. Mama was two years older, so they would have had to have continued their romance years after she graduated. I have always been told that nobody knew mama was pregnant until she started screaming with stomach pain. Someone in the family ran to Cousin Hartie and returned with her to help figure out why mama was writhing in pain and clenching her stomach. Cousin Hartie surprised everyone when she announced mama was in labor!

I suppose after that, it was a chaotic scene. I was delivered right there at home. So many women died in childbirth in those days, especially poor Blacks. Mama and I both lived without any medical intervention. I believe God breathed strong will and determination to survive into my lungs on that cold winter night. He knew the struggles I would endure. Artie Lee, named after Cousin Hartie, (maybe) the impromptu midwife. My middle name is the same as Madea's. I believe mama had told Bobby, and he had not taken it well, to say the least.

Sometimes the mind escapes reality due to psychological illness, but other times it's simply denial, and I'm not referring to a river in Egypt. I empathize with the turmoil, and the loneliness mama had to have felt, even with such a large family. In Black families, the unwritten rule is what happens at home stays at home. Any dysfunction or debilitating situations are close to the chest. Well, that's been the truth for as long as I can remember.

Some of my favorite shows are court tv, forensic files, or cold case types. I never thought I would be investigating myself. I really thought I had all my facts straight and knew precisely where to point my blaming finger. I present Cold Case #12141960: *What Happened to Me from 1966- 1974.*

Healing comes from truth and accountability. I am accepting this mission to reveal and unravel each layer of hidden information, thereby helping to begin the process of eliminating harmful generational curses. This family and many others around the world are built on her. Pretense and secrecy rob generations of blood-related people of the full benefits of familial love and support, a necessary component of well-developed maturation.

Mama was a small-framed woman, which makes it almost unrealistic her belly was not visible. How could she hide a full-term pregnancy without detection? Her high school graduation picture clearly shows her delicate facial features and elongated neck, and she was not "big-boned." Yet, at any given time, at least ten pairs of eyes were looking at her, and not one of them noticed a bump? My intuition tells me that dog don't bark, a country way of saying something is off with that story.

Transparency is the main pathway to healing, family unity, and truth. I begrudgingly regret the lack of knowledge about my ancestry and any valuable information withheld in that regard. Unfortunately, memories fade or become more selective, so personal memory alone is unreliable. My sources for credible information are from my stark memory, aunts, uncle's recollections, Wikipedia, public records, obituaries, death certificates, and *Ancestry.com*. I hoped to clarify any misconceptions I had developed while focusing on my own agenda.

Years of missing information has prevented me from fully understanding how the missteps in responsibility occurred repeatedly. The destruction of the Black family structure originated long before my birth. Like many generations before me, fathers, and some mothers, have abandoned their children and never looked back.

Jana, mama's oldest brother, about two years younger than mama, gives quite a different sequence of events.

I asked, "Do you remember or know who delivered me, and was it a surprise?"

He paused and replied, "I don't want to make you mad."

I encouraged him to go on. How could I be angry? On the contrary, I am grateful to whoever it was. I could hear the hesitation in his voice as he slowly said, "It wasn't a woman that delivered you." I quickly thought he was going to say it was him.

Jana slowly said, "It was a man named Nehemiah Williams. He was in the military and was the only one who knew what to do when Sis (my mama) went into labor. He was a medic in the army, so he cut the cord."

Sister is mama's oldest sister. Country folks love coming up with nicknames.

He said Nehemiah lived in Houston and that he may still be alive. Jana is one of the most reliable truthful men you will ever meet, and at nearly eighty years old, his memory is still sharp. All I could say was, "Wow!" I had never heard that. He went on to say that the only surprise was the labor, not the pregnancy, as I already suspected. Stevie Wonder could see they were pretending to be blind.

Bobby and Jana were also friends, both graduating from high school just months before my birth. He said that Bobby moved to Dallas after graduation but often came back to Bullard to see us for a couple of years, then they didn't see him again after that. Jana believed Cousin Hartie frequently came to check on mama afterward but certainly did not cut my umbilical cord. He thought that possibly out of gratitude, mama had named me after her. Now that's a more believable reenactment.

Through *Ancestry.com*, I located Nehemiah E. Williams in Houston. He was born in 1933. He would have been twenty-seven when he sprang into action and safely ushered me into the world. His tombstone verifies he served in the Korean war; undoubtedly, he would have emergency medical training. Everything Jana told me checked out. Nehemiah passed away in Houston, Texas, in 2016. Stories like mine are what movies are made of. An infamous Black Korean war vet delivers a baby after fighting for a country that has turned its back on the black race. His military duties and nearly losing his life meant nothing. How amazing, if true. He is a hero in every sense of the word. Nehemiah lived to be eighty-three years old. I imagine him being well-liked for many more generous acts of kindness like that.

That prompted me to google the book of Nehemiah in the Bible. Nehemiah 8:10 is the first entry Nehemiah said, "Go and enjoy choice food and sweet drinks, and send some to those who have nothing prepared. This day is holy to our Lord. Do not grieve for the joy of the Lord is your strength."

That is a befitting scripture for a bastard child born into poverty. Clearly, there were no preparations for my arrival and no expectations for my future. God has a purpose for my life and prepared a place for me in the bleakest of situations. I am ashamed to say, until now, I had not taken the time to walk in mama's shoes and truly understand the pain she silently carried. The toll on her mental state was apparent, but it was unaddressed and ignored.

She was very reserved and selfless. I believe she could never genuinely blossom into her own true identity due to a series of unfortunate life occurrences. A grown-ass woman deserved to be called by her birth name. Josephine is of French origin, meaning "Jehovah increases." But she remained simply Sis, increasingly becoming invisible.

Jana told me, "Somebody gave Sis an apple. It had something in it that messed up her mind. She was a young girl when it happened. People used to put voodoo on folks back in the day. I can't remember how old she was, but after that, she always had fits."

That's what they called any type of psychosis in those days. So, it was either they had a "fit," or the person in question had a "nervous breakdown." Is that the same thing that happened to Cinderella? Regardless, that bad apple did not hinder her from graduating on time with her class in 1958.

Being a single mother in those days was taboo. She was not considered respectful. The pressure of being judged and the betrayal from Bobby may have led to frequent long-term stays at Rusk State Hospital, where she was eventually diagnosed with schizophrenia. It was easy to get diagnosed with schizophrenia back in those days, especially if you were Black. Black oppression comes in many forms. Institutional imprisonment is just a step down from being enslaved, shackled, and tied down against your will. It probably wasn't wise to act out too many times; you might end up getting electric shock treatments in a straitjacket.

I asked Sister her version one more time, and this is her reply, "A midwife delivered you. It wasn't no damn Nehemiah, and Sis didn't eat no damn poison apple. Madea rubbed saltpeter in the top of Sis's head. She said it was her nature that made her act out like that."

"Nature?" I asked.

Sister said, "I didn't understand what she meant at the time. I just remember her saying that."

It was an odd conversation for a mother to have with a child, especially in those days, but hey, I wasn't there. Mental illness was something of a mystery during those days. Most illnesses were prayed away, and some type of home remedy was used if needed.

These confusing yet compelling versions of mama's past unearth the reasoning behind her passive, somewhat withdrawn character. Jana shared with me happier times when they were kids, playing in the fields having tomato fights, and how he had accidentally hit mama in the face with a green tomato. They had been splattering each other with ripe ones. He said his shirt was covered in tomato seeds when Madea whipped him. Then, still smiling, he recanted, "Sis was a lot of fun before she ate that apple."

Regardless, reading between the lines, whether it was some form of abuse, a poisonous apple, or a metabolic disorder, something happened to change her normal childish behavior. Ironically, the same damn thing happened to me. Also, during her developmental years, she lost a baby brother, John Edd. Again, according to *Ancestry.com*, he was about six months old when he died. Mama would have been about four years old, clearly old enough to understand and grieve his loss. That had to be a devastating event for a four-year-old.

By 1950, Madea had six more children, making it almost impossible to lend emotional support to them all and still work the fields to help feed the family. Being emotionally fragile and the oldest, a lot more was expected of mama than her younger siblings. According to court records, to add to a list of unfortunate circumstances, Bobby married in August 1963. Hearing that news had to have been unbearable.

Madea's health began to decline, rendering her bedfast by her early forties. Another blow to mama's stability happened when Madea passed away in 1965. I can feel the anxiety, loneliness, and uncertainty mama had to have felt. Yet, silently, stoically, never complaining, never asking for help, she endured it all. We are quick to say, "If that were me, chile, I woulda—" The truth of the matter is, it all depends on one's resources and/or mental fortitude. I understand the true meaning of what being beaten down means, and strength is subjective.

Mama's life was crumbling around her. She truly needed someone in her corner, providing her unconditional love, protection, and respect. Unfortunately, broken women are attracted to those who pretend to love them. Pretending is a critical element in generational curses which I too learned the art of pretending very well from adults, as they pretended to raise me properly. I mimicked the same behavior by acting as they did.

In many ways, I am glad to say I raised myself. I taught myself the finest words. I firmly believe in their proper use. "You know Sis have them fits." I mean, really, where did those terms come from? Mama had a mental illness. The correct terminology is schizophrenia. Although postpartum depression was not a consideration at that time, I believe that also played a part in her frame of mind.

Schizophrenia weighs heavily on people who suffer from

it and on the people who love those suffering from it. Dealing with the symptoms and medication challenges makes it an exceptionally demanding illness for everyone involved. Schizophrenia is a mental illness that interferes with thinking clearly, seeing reality from fantasy, and making decisions. It also can make it difficult for some people to manage emotions and relate to others.

There is no single cause of schizophrenia. Research shows it may result from many factors, including an imbalance of certain chemicals in the brain. No one fully understands why some people get schizophrenia. We know it's definitely not the fault of the person diagnosed with the disease. But since more than 2.4 million Americans today have this illness, you're not alone.

Symptoms of schizophrenia can include hallucinations, delusions, paranoia, and withdrawal from family and friends. Hearing voices, seeing things, or sensing things that aren't there. Delusions mean to believe something is true or real that's false to other people. It also includes paranoia or being unusually suspicious.

Right now, there is no cure for schizophrenia, but it is treatable. Many people successfully manage the disease through a combination of medications, counseling, and a support system. A diagnosis doesn't change who you are. Just as a person diagnosed with cancer isn't just a cancer patient, someone diagnosed with schizophrenia is more than just a disease.

Simply put, a strong support system, and consistent medical care, would have made all the difference in the world for us all. I understand mama didn't ask for help, but the pain she felt was visible to anyone claiming to love her. Over time it was hidden by a dense fog, with zero visibility. Her world became darker with each passing day, and that shroud of darkness covered me as well. We desperately need one strong hand to reach for us.

Pastor's Bastard

Nicely put, I was a love child
Illegitimate; naturally wild,
Blissfully hidden, an underhanded conception...
Mindless deception.
You're not going to marry mama?
Oh! Is fatherhood too much drama?
Your family was better than...
They encouraged you to be less than,
A man.
You didn't see fit giving me your name.
For that, you should be ashamed.
The Lord called you to preach.
For me, you would not reach.
Laying healing hands on folks.
All the while, your baby girl needed strokes.

CHAPTER 2

BIG TOE INTRO

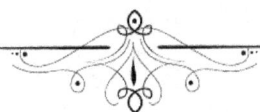

Nineteen sixty-six was my first encounter with my new "daddy." It was right before my sixth birthday in December. Not that birthdays were celebrated in any unique way, but it's etched into my mind when I no longer felt safe. According to court documents, mama married him precisely one week before my sixth birthday. There were no presents for me, just the presence of a new family member. They happily exchanged wedding vows after a short courtship. They vowed to love, honor, and cherish, for better, for worse, for richer, for poorer, in sickness and health, till death do them apart. Apparently, he had two fingers intertwined behind his back.

Mama was twenty-six at the time but still very immature and naive due to limited life experiences. She was an easy mark for a person pretending to love her. Daddy was not the leader and protector he should have been. The breakdown in my family structure is deep-rooted. Generation upon generation of black men shirking their responsibilities, sadly sometimes because they haven't seen an example. When a child is caught doing something wrong, the first thing said is, "Where is his/ her mama at?"

Birth records show my stepdad was only twenty years old but already very manipulative and deceptive. He honed in on Mama's quiet demeanor and her visible meekness. Seeing that she was a single mother of a small child made her all the more attractive to him. It didn't take long before he realized that my real daddy had excused himself of all responsibility for my well-being. He had wholly removed himself from the situation. We were left to sink or swim. Bobby was not interested in who was taking his place because he had another family now. Mama just had to suck it up and move on, so she did just that. Her options were limited, with only a high school education and no source of income. Marriage for her was her only way out.

She was doing what was expected of her. She was no different than any other young woman starting her future. But, of course, she anticipated a better life. I believe she thought he would also love, protect, and cherish her. Mama didn't have a mean bone in her body. Had he loved her, and comforted her, and matched her true love, I wouldn't be typing my testimony. But, instead, he hid his evilness until she felt trapped.

Soon after their marriage, Mama packed our meager belongings, and off we went to start our new fake family. I remember we were driving away. Daddy (my grandfather) yelled, "He will have both of you before long. You mark my words." He always had an ill-fated retort ending with "You mark my word." Daddy was a foul-mouthed, negative, unhappy man. He wasn't one to beat around the bush. He spoke his mind without hesitation, especially after a few swigs of whiskey. But on this day, he had bided his tongue.

Daddy had tantrums that included but were not limited to cursing, throwing objects, and spewing hateful prophecies at whoever was the unfortunate offspring that day. Nonchalantly, he claimed to foresee danger for me at the hands of mama's new husband. He, in an instant, relinquished all responsibility, washed his hands of us as if we were strangers. He did nothing to protect us, whether he was citing facts or speculation. Instead, he coldly watched us drive away. Why didn't he yell? "If you harm the hair on their heads, I'm coming for you, you son-of-a-bitch!" I had heard him cursing aggressively many times until the veins on the side of his neck swelled, and spit was flying out of his mouth.

It seems he wanted to prove he was right at my expense. Instead of farewell wishes, he seemed to be telling us to go to hell! I had no clue what he meant at that time, but it didn't take long for me to figure it out. He knew something we didn't know about this man. Yet, he did nothing to intervene. In short, that is precisely what happened. He had both of us in his bed. Every night for a few years, I slept in bed between them. Mama obeyed and did not cross him.

I remember the first time he touched me inappropriately. It wasn't a touch but more of a hard nudge between my legs. I was sleeping soundly at the foot of the bed they were sharing. Suddenly I was startled awake by something pushing forcefully between my legs. He was cramming his big toe into me. I sprang up to a sitting position, wide-eyed and confused. My eyes met

19

his, glaring at me and grinning. He put his finger to his mouth, "Shhh, yo' mama sleepin'."

Mama was peacefully asleep in his arms. He kissed her forehead and pulled her closer to himself while continuing to glare at me. His big, jagged teeth looked like they had never been introduced to a toothbrush. I was frozen with fear and a feeling of uncertainty that a child should never have to feel. That was the first of many indecent acts he forced upon me. Without uttering a sound, he had intimidated me thoroughly. After that, he always kept us apart in some way or another. If I even thought about telling mama what happened, he was always nearby redirecting or interjecting while glaring at me in an attempt to instill fear.

Of course, I was afraid of him. At only six years old, I had already dealt with some harsh realities. I realized he was an evil and dishonest man. I think I even understood he was pretending to love mama. It was a game. The way he kissed her while glaring at me. He relished in her vulnerabilities and her false sense of security. He was making her feel loved again, all the while showing me his true intent, to frighten and intimidate. He flaunted deception and disgusting behavior in a way that mama didn't realize what he was up to initially. Once again, she was hoodwinked by a man pretending to love her. This time, he also pretended to love her child. Double deception, with his right hand, raised to Jesus!

Sleep for me was restless and interrupted. It usually finally came after sure exhaustion, from pushing his hands away over and over again. At the same time, he touched places that really weren't meant to be touched yet, in that way. Inhaling the toxic odors from his breath and body always made my stomach do backflips. I would stiffen my body and hold my breath until sure fatigue took over. That is how I often drifted to sleep, making it impossible ever entirely to relax. His sinister grin taunted me in my dreams and waited for me when I awoke.

There were times I screamed, "I'm telling Daddy what you do to me!"

That only made him laugh. "I'm your daddy now."

I vowed never to call him daddy, ever. I yelled, "You are not my daddy!"

He pressed his hand firmly over my mouth and nose, "Don't you talk back, gal," pushing my chin upward until I stumbled.

Mama did not utter a sound. By then, she had to have concluded that she had made a colossal mistake marrying him.

I looked up at him and sternly stated, "I will not call you daddy. I already have one!"

Mama yelled for me to stop talking back. She would then softly say, "He is your stepdaddy," with a sad expression. "You have to listen to him."

From that day, I referred to him as *He*. After that, I wanted nothing to do with him.

The urban dictionary definition for stepdad is a guy willing to hook up with a woman with children from a previous relationship. Some step kids will love him, and others will not. The step-kids real dad is not in the picture. If a kid is lucky, their mother will find a good stepdad and not some jerk that treats them like crap. Ironically that's exactly the step-jerk mama chose. Not all stepdads are mean, abusive, or child molesters. Some stepdads step in and step up positively, wanting the absolute best for the mother and the children.

Their marriage was a missed opportunity for greatness. He had the chance to improve our lives, but instead, he took advantage of an already broken woman and her child. Seeing that mama was already in a dark place, his personal goal was to grind her down further. This man looked at a five-year-old little girl and planned to destroy her. Helping me become strong, confident, and loved was furthest from his mind. Mama's husband intended to demoralize and crush my ego. His actions only hindered my natural childhood development and crippled my emotions and spirit. He anticipated he would break me by keeping me afraid and uncertain of my safety. I am here to report I have been bent and twisted, but proudly stand with a sane mind to deliver a message of hope and resiliency.

If only he had treated mama with love, respect, and dignity, I believe she would have been able to step into her true self and find her purpose. She didn't need fancy clothes or diamonds. Mama was satisfied with a very simple life. All she ever wanted was to be treated with love and respect. Had he honored their wedding vows, she would have been content with that. Instead, dreams and aspirations she may have had for her future, she put them aside and mastered disguising her true feelings.

When I was growing up, a child was not allowed to speak out of turn; if an adult didn't initiate the conversation, there was no conversation to be had. God forbid you were caught "looking in grown folk's mouth" while they talked. So getting a word in edgewise was challenging to say the least. He was well aware of my constraint when trying to start up a conversation. All he had to do was give me that mean look, and I would cower.

Before he came along, I can't remember ever getting a spanking, meaning it wasn't memorable, like a beating. I was free to play and enjoy being a kid, making mud pies, and chasing grasshoppers. Not once do I recall being fearful or scared to express myself. At Daddy's house, I was included. No one mistreated me, they loved me, and I felt it. Thankfully I had those memories to cling to. At six years old, I unquestionably understood he was horrible. He would hurt me when Mama was not paying attention. Though I was too young to perceive the future, I knew we were in big trouble.

After being awakened with a big toe between my legs, he was constantly smacking me wherever his hard crusty hand landed on my tiny body, pushing me, or cursing at me for no reason. Mama either ignored the abuse or would not intervene, giving him all the power he commanded without interference from anyone. For damn sure, Bobby was not looking back. Mama desperately needed a strong support system. She quietly witnessed each of her younger siblings leave her behind. The grooming process had begun, in the name of love.

Violation Education

Inside?

Me?

Really?

Probing, cramming, and violating me?

Frightening me every night.

You had no right!

With your dirty fingers and that crusty big toe...

Crippling a little girl's ego.

Teaching me to trust no one,

Playing stepdad was just a con.

All the while, you smiled,

Perfectly pleased to hurt a child.

From your weakness, I draw strength.

Now I know my relevance.

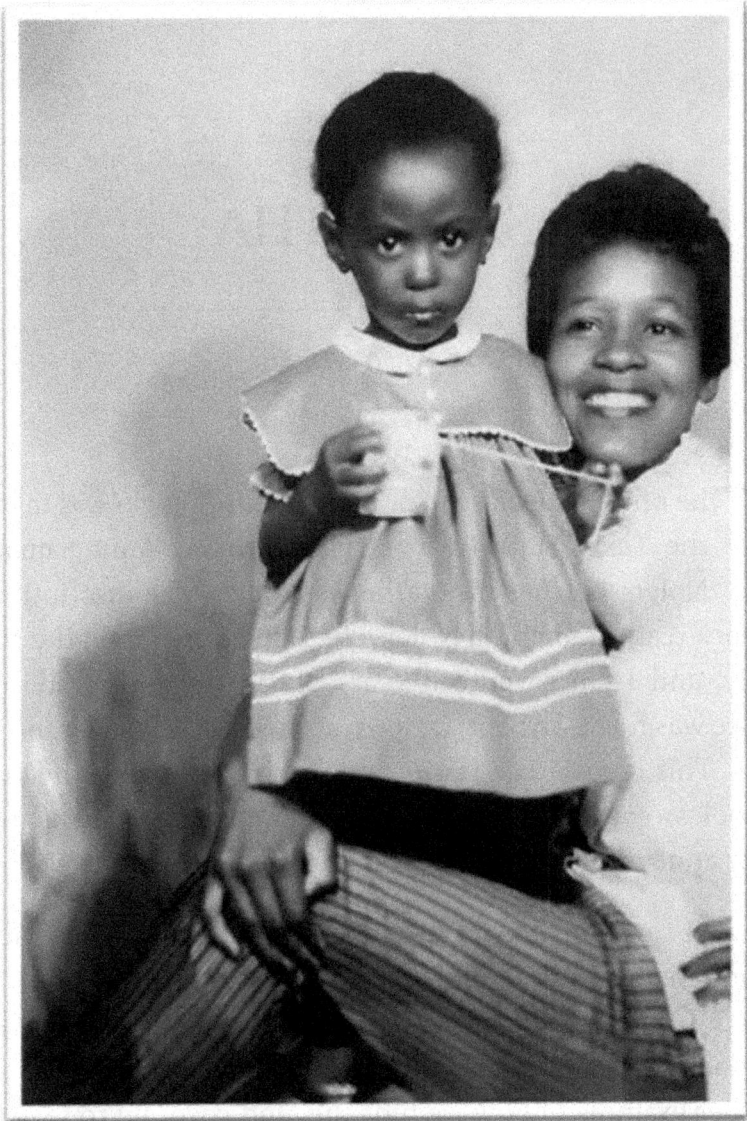

CHAPTER 3

SAMANTHA

The only thing close to a "baby picture" I own was taken at the Texas State Fair in Tyler with my Aunt Samantha Nolen, but her nickname was Mack. The inscription on the back read: "Samantha Nolen, she is the third girl in the Nolen family, and I am seventeen years old in the 10th grade. This picture was made on Sept. 12, 1963, at the East Texas Fair in Tyler, Texas. This is Artie Lee Jessie, and she is two years old. Doesn't she look sweet to you?" Pardon her grammatical errors. I appear pretty annoyed, actually, but just as sweet as she portrayed.

At seventeen, Mack attempted to hide my illegitimacy by memorializing the picture with lies. Jessie is the name I was denied. It makes me think of the movie *Joe Dirt*. In it, Joe says, "My daddy wasn't there to take me to the fair, cuz he didn't care." Another example of how we hide, lie, and cover up to save face. For the record, my name at birth was Nolen, my mama's maiden name, and it is Nolen still today.

Mack **advocated for my emotional well-being and**

dignity even back then. Knowing Bobby had married, Mack wanted it to appear that he had done right by me as well. Mack stepped up for my absent parents; mama's presence was sporadic due to her mental condition. She was a fixer, always wanting to make life as grand as possible, regardless of how destitute the family became.

I recall Ruth and Renebabe, my mother's youngest sisters crying out, cursing Daddy for leaving us without an adequate food supply. I had to be around four years old. I remember us three together hungry, crying in desperation. The older siblings had left Bullard. I would have no way of knowing where mama was, but I can assume she was away for treatment.

It was the kind of hunger that when you finally eat, it's hard to swallow because your mouth and tongue are dry from the lack of a reason to produce saliva. Then, after what seemed like days of your stomach stuck to your spine, something totally unappetizing, like some nasty elbow macaroni that looked like giant fat white worms in cloudy water appeared. I cried, "I don't want it!" That may have been the only choice at the moment.

I was willing to wait for syrup on a biscuit. Homemade biscuits was the only food that put a smile on my face. The sweet, comforting aroma of biscuits cooking gets my attention every time. I would be overjoyed if I were lucky enough to have some sorghum syrup. Mama used to tell me I was so tiny when I was a baby that I could fit in a syrup bucket. But frequently, it was biscuits and sugar syrup. Sugar syrup consists of water and a lot of white sugar. Bring it to a boil until it thickens, pour it on the biscuit, and breakfast is served. I absolutely hated beans of any kind. The musty smell of them boiling on the stove would make me gag. Mack would sit at the table with me, almost begging me to eat them, until I puked on her. Nobody tried making me eat beans after that.

Pete, another of mama's brothers confided, "Daddy was a poor provider; he worked out of town doing construction jobs, rarely sent money home, and when he returned home, I would hear Madea giving him hell because he would come home empty-handed. We all had to work to get a little food and clothes. Jana and I had to take care of Ruth and Renebabe after Madea passed. Madea received a check every month for her disability, and we no longer had that little money. It was really tough. We hardly went to school because we had to work in the fields to help feed the family. That's why Mack didn't graduate until she was almost twenty. I barely graduated myself."

Jana had neglected to mention the around-the-clock attention Madea required in the last days of her life. Multiple Sclerosis (MS) had crippled her, making her dependent on Daddy and her children for her basic personal needs. Knowing Mack's caring nature, she undoubtedly missed school to care for Madea also. Yet, she maintained her fun-loving personality through all the grief and poverty.

When I was about five, she said I could touch the sky if I kept walking across the field. "You see the clouds down there behind the trees? Keep walking until you get behind the trees, and you can touch the sky."

We would start walking, but she always found a reason to go back to the house. She always had a funny song to sing or point out imaginary objects in the clouds on the way back. Whatever she imagined, I imagined as well. Mack bought my first

Dr. Seuss books. She read a lot to me. One of her favorites was *Green Eggs and Ham* because the main character's name is Sam. We would recite excerpts from the book "I do not like them, Sam-I-Am. I do not like green eggs and ham."

All that fun ended for me when she got married as well. Jana too had married a couple years prior. His two stepdaughters and I were flower girls in Mack's wedding at Corinth Baptist Church. Mack happily moved away with her new husband. At six years old, my life headed on a further downward spiral. That occasion marked a new beginning for me as well.

Mack made me promise to do well in school and stressed the importance. She said, "When you get book sense, nobody can take that from you." I didn't fully understand, but I got the gist of it... do well in school. I would start first grade in the fall. Mack said, "Make all A's, and I'll send you something pretty." I didn't care about that. I wanted her to stay and play with me forever. Mack surprised me with a box of new pretty dresses that came in the mail to start the first grade. She continued this tradition each school year.

Beautiful new dresses and white ribbon-trimmed socks filled the box. The distinct aroma of new fabric and the crispness of the materials gave me anxiety and happiness at the same time. I anticipated some form of mental torture related to my visible satisfaction. He didn't enjoy seeing a smile on any face. When the packages arrived, he would oversee the emptying of the contents. Occasionally, he would burn them fresh out of the box after making me think I could keep them. He would say, "I don't see nothing for nobody else." Other times He would allow me to keep them. Saying, "Don't make me have to burn'em." As if I had any say in the matter.

Keeping the box depended on his mood when the box showed up, whether or not I kept some, all, or none. So, I kept a poker face, not allowing him the satisfaction of checking my face to see which garment delighted me most. "Oh, you like that one?" Then he would make me watch it go up in flames in a wood-burning stove. I had to rely on happy memories, and I held on to them repeatedly when I needed a mental escape.

Like when Mack said, "Hey Lee, you believe I can make that bull jump the fence?" Wide-eyed and heart-pounding at the thought of it, I said, "How?"

She directed me to stay on the porch. She jumped down off the porch with a red fabric. The bull belonged to a neighboring farmer that didn't live on the grounds. As with any other quiet night in the country, not much was stirring except mosquitos and fireflies. The deafening silence and tranquility were too much for Mack. She craved excitement. The bull was busy grazing on grass, minding his own business until Mack began snarling and aggressively waving that red fabric.

The bull started digging his hooves into the ground, kicking up dust and looking straight at Mack. I was shaking and begging her to stop. Sure enough, the angry bull jumped the barbed wire fence and charged toward Mack. We both screamed as she ran inside, both she and the bull kicking up dust; she swiftly closed the door. We laughed until our sides ached. Times like those sustained me and provided countless hours of pleasurable daydreaming. Mack instilled hope, inspiration, and vivid imagination in me without preconceived notions of its lasting impression.

Samantha Annette Nolen (Mack) graduated in May 1966. She looked beautiful with a bow in her hair. Her class yearbook was displayed on *Ancestry.com*. I was able to catch a glimpse of her personality and the types of activities she entertained. I was amazed by her tenacity in not giving up regardless of how far behind she became while helping support her family. Madea's passing may have given her the ambition needed to keep trudging onward, speaking to the strong woman she became, committed to family unconditionally.

She was described in the caption as an excellent dancer; she was a member of the ER-Ra-Go Go Dance Club. Mack loved music and dancing for sure. She could turn the simplest thing into something silly. Mack knew the importance of laughter. She undoubtedly knew she possessed an outgoing personality and was willing literally to share it with the less fortunate.

She taught me nursery rhymes, and we would sing and play for hours. Our favorite song with hand slaps was Miss Merry Mack's nursery rhyme. Mack's bright light would be a beacon of hope in the years to come. For every unpleasant experience, I simultaneously tried to replace it with a pleasant memory, most of which began and ended with Mack. Maya Angelou states, "Be a rainbow in somebody else's cloud." Mack was that for me, a vividly bright rainbow.

I can't recall how many came (the aunts) to take mama and me to see Pete off. He'd been drafted into the army. I remember the kerfuffle, resulting in mama and me not being a part of the send-off. There was a lot of yelling, cursing, pushing, and hitting. My mother's husband had given a clear message that we were his property and couldn't go anywhere without his permission; he always had the final say.

Some months passed, and Mack asked to take me to see James Brown in concert, about thirty minutes away in Tyler. Without a quarrel, he permitted it. Willie Ray, Mack's new husband, was with her. Maybe facing them caused him to back down. Mack had brought fresh clothes for me to wear. I was shaking with excitement to be leaving with her. She kept telling me how pretty I was. There was no way I could ruin her opinion of me. Truthfully, I felt dirty and ugly. Besides, I didn't want him to mess Mack up, too.

An announcer's voice came over the loudspeaker, "Ladies and gentlemen, put your hands together with the King of Soul, Mr. James Brown!" He was sweating, spinning around, and screaming into the microphone. I had never experienced anything of that magnitude. The bright lights, loud music, a massive crowd of people singing and dancing in an outdoor stadium were intoxicating. For a short while, I could forget about home. I could imagine this night lasting forever. Smells from the concession stand in the air reminded me of the tasteless food at home. But Mack had not forgotten about me, so, for now, I enjoyed every minute of the concert.

Undeniably it was a conscious effort on her part to do whatever she could to show me a better life. Mack always seemed so happy. I wanted to be just like her, nicely dressed, happy, and singing. James Brown belted out, "Say it loud. I'm Black I'm Proud, Say it loud..."

Approaching seven years old, I recall thinking to myself, yes, *I am black, but what is proud?*

"Say it loud, I'm black and I'm proud!" The crowd went wild. The blacks were chanting, fists pumping in the air, and dancing, while the white people seemed uncomfortable, and some began to leave. Unaware at the time of the significance of the song. James Brown himself, a civil rights advocate, was using his platform to encourage Blacks to love themselves and their God-given black skin.

James Brown used his musical gift to help advance the black power movement. He wrote the song himself after the assassination of Dr. Martin Luther King Jr. I was unaware of the fight for racial equality. I was fighting for childhood equality— my own. My fundamental rights are to blossom uninhibited, play, and grow without being held back in any way, and live without fear. I have the right to feel black, beautiful, and proud. I didn't know that feeling yet, and if *He* had any say, I would never be proud of myself or anything life has to offer.

The dictionary defines proud as having or showing a high or excessively high opinion of oneself or one's importance. I felt none of that, but Mack had a way of making me feel like I mattered. She gave me hugs, told me I was beautiful, and called me smart.

"Do good in school, Lee. I love you."

I held onto her until she peeled me off. "Please take me with you," I cried. "Please don't leave me here!"

"I'll be back soon," she whispered in my ear.

He stood quietly observing, taking it all in, enjoying seeing me beg and plead.

Composing this chapter about Mack's influence on my life made me think about how everybody had another name. The one on the birth certificate was a technicality. How did Samantha turn to Mack? I never thought to ask. It invalidates the person, another pretense, not acknowledging their entire existence. A nickname is a substitute for the proper name, but there comes a time to put some respect on it and get it correct.

No sooner than they pulled away, with a wide stance, arms folded, those jagged yellow teeth showing, he was in my face yelling, "Shut the hell up before I give you something to cry about. Get ready for bed!"

Mama said nothing as usual. A bittersweet word *soon* whispered in my ear by my aunt would be a long time, even if it were just a day. A day in my life already felt like an eternity. The feelings of love from Mack sustained me until we connected again. Everything about her excited me and gave me hope.

As expected, at seven years old, I started first grade. Just as Mack had, learning to read and write brought color to my life. I remember my first books. Dick and Jane reading books. I loved reading. Mack had encouraged me to do well, and I did not want to let her down. I understood school was important to her, so it was also important to me. I lived to make her proud because one thing I knew for sure, she cared about me.

Eating in the cafeteria was not my favorite. All the food on the tray had to be consumed before returning the tray. The food was a hundred times better than what I had at home, but I was still picky. I would drink the milk then fill the carton with whatever I didn't like. I would push the milk carton down to appear empty; they never caught on. Otherwise, I would have gotten a good spanking from the teacher. In those days, if you got a spanking by an adult, you got another one at home.

I want to make a clarification, a spanking is a hand to buttocks action. I have never experienced one of those as a disciplinary measure. I got whippings, all over my body after having to fetch my own "piss elm pole." School was a safe haven, and there would be no bad reports for me. I was eager to learn. It was a welcomed distraction from what was happening back at the ranch.

Samantha originated as a Biblical name. Samantha means listener of God. Ironically that meaning fits her perfectly. Of course, without a doubt, she would have done more than listen had I spoken up sooner. I believe she would have put the fear of God in him had she known, but I was afraid and ashamed. I thought I was sparing her feelings and was worried he may also run her away.

Mama

*I'm yo' mama, but I can't protect **you**.*

I'm yo' mama, but, motherly, untrue.

I'm yo' mama, but I am so beaten down.

I'm yo' mama, but I no longer wear a crown.

I'm yo' mama but I can't tuck you in at night.

I'm your mother, but I'm having a hard time doing what's right.

Please forgive me,

Mama

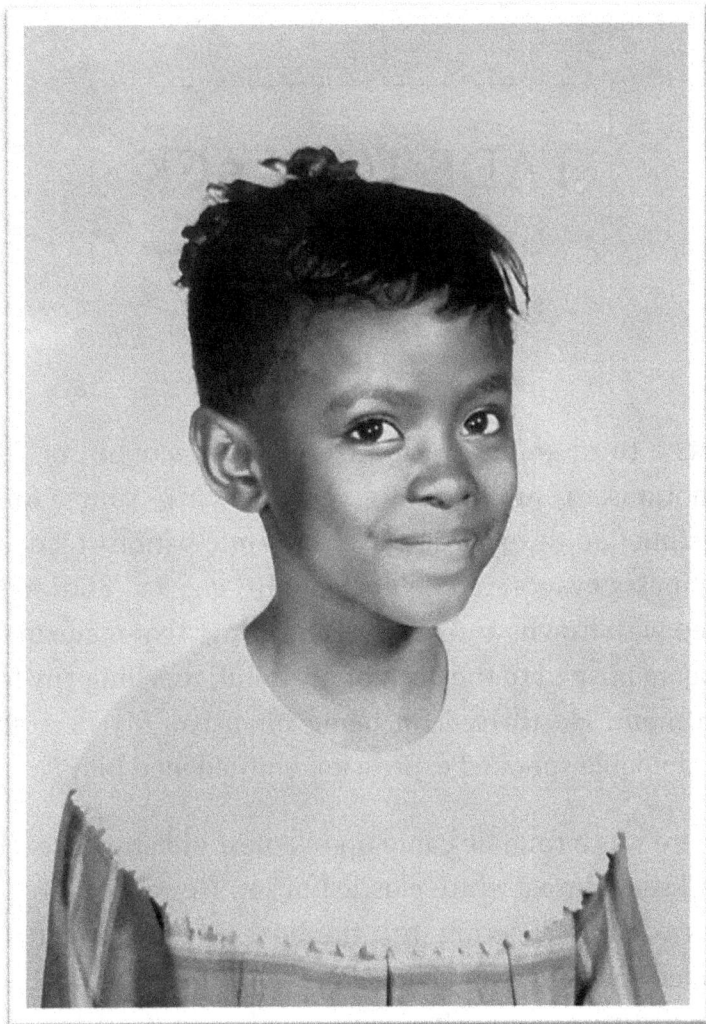

CHAPTER 4

FADE TO BLACK

I was a third grader, with a tremendous amount of pent-up emotions, resulting from experiencing some form of dysfunction, sexual trauma, or the anticipation of it daily. My childishness evaporated quickly. My giggles and silliness, replaced with frowns and fear. All the things that made me smile were being pushed to the back of my mind, repelling any form of contentment. He thrived on being offensive. My nervousness, and undeniable spooked expression emboldened him.

There was a time he came upon a nest of baby mice. He had scooped them into a white plastic bucket. He yelled, "Come look at what I found." Peering into the bucket, I saw about six tiny pink mice squirming and squeaking with their tiny voices. Still, in their disturbed nest. They looked so helpless. All of a sudden, he doused them with bleach! The pungent smell choked me. I began gagging, backing away in disbelief, about to puke.

He, on the other hand found it to be quite amusing. He covered his mouth, fake swallowing his laughter. He was having the time of his life. His eyes were wide and glowing, overpowering mice with toxic bleach fumes while sending a clear message to me. He demonstrated how easily he could end life, innocent babies' lives at that. I could tell it made him happy to see me so frightened. So it is very safe to say that the smell of bleach always triggers that memory from about eight years old.

He worked at a lumberyard when he wasn't tormenting something or someone. I know that because he would make me help him load his truck with scrap wood. He would bring it home to burn to warm the house in the winter. His hard work paid off. One fine morning he proudly proclaimed we were going to see where he would build us a new house. Then, speaking directly at me with his shit-eating grin, "Gal can have her own room." I didn't own the skin I was in. He really meant there would be a wall between mama and me. I owned nothing but what I kept inside my head. Mama nodded pleasingly with a half-grin.

Mama gathered up my baby sister, and off we went to see the land where *He* would build us a house. As we turned onto the dirt road, I was shocked to see us heading toward daddy's house. Mama looked puzzled as well but kept quiet.

Just before we approached daddy's house, he pulled the truck off the road to the right and parked, "I'mma build us a house. Y'all gone have to help." As far as the eyes could see, there was tall grass and weeds. "Soon as we clear a spot, I'mma build us a nice house. Told ya' I'mma make you a room. You'll be all by yourself," he smugly cheesed at me.

I understood the innuendo, so did mama as she shamefully looked away, pretending to take in the rugged terrain. How the

39

hell could he construct a house here? I would soon find out. That summer seemed to last a year. I would start fourth grade overworked and tired. He worked me from sunup to sundown on his days off, which seemed to be too often. We primitively cleared the land. He didn't own one damn power tool.

Regardless of his profoundly flawed personality, he was productive. He used all the tools in his arsenal. He was able to work a day job while meticulously building a house to shelter and destroy his own family. He wasn't at all lazy. I was always awake long before the rooster crowed. So when he yelled, "Get up, Gal, we got work to do!" I was fully dressed, but I still took my sweet time. I always wore as many clothes as I could to bed to help ward off his wandering hands.

Shadowing his every move, I observed his disgusting hands selecting a small tree branch. Then, holding it in the shape of a large Y, he strolled across the land. "This is how you find water." He walked holding a damn stick like he was privy to some special information from the ground on well digging. "You see how the stick is starting to point down. I could see him aim the stick toward the ground. "Water is here!"

I looked at him, thinking to myself, "I don't give a damn about any of it. I'd much rather die of thirst."

"Yeah, we can dig right here."

Who the hell is we? He grabbed the post hole diggers and started digging wildly. Deeper and deeper, he searched until he was standing inside a huge hole in the ground. He would send a bucket of dirt up to me on a long rope, and I would dump it and lower the bucket back down to him. After about a hundred buckets of dirt, I quickly understood the meaning of we.

Sometimes I accidentally dropped it. I only got lucky and hit him once or twice. My ass was beaten or abused regardless if I did nothing to deserve it. I congratulated any rare occasion to get the tiniest catharsis. I was a helpless nine-year-old. There was not much I could physically do to him. I imagined burying him in the well.

I started singing to myself. *"There was some dirt. The prettiest dirt that you ever did see. That you ever did see. And in that dirt. And in that dirt. There was a hole. The prettiest hole. The prettiest hole that you ever did see. That you ever did see. And in that hole. There was a man. The meanest man. The meanest man. That you ever did see. That you ever did see. And on that man. And on that man. Was all the dirt—"*

I heard him yelling, "Hurry up, gal! What you doin' up there?"

I googled finding water with a stick, and there it was. It is called water dousing. It is the practice of using a forked stick or similar device to locate underground water, minerals, or other hidden or lost substances for hundreds of years. The person who is dousing holds the stick and walks around a property, hoping the stick will dip or twitch when he walks over the underground water. He would have hit water if the stick had dipped any place he aimed it, as so stated in the article. Praise God, let there be water.

A huge truck arrived to deliver and install big cement cylinders into the hole to keep it from caving in and minimizing the effects of drinking nasty well water. He had accomplished what he sat out to do. He had provided water for the family. Now the building of the house could begin. Building the family home was another failed attempt at greatness. This could have been a collaboration of ideas from us all to be a great start. A nice kitchen, a vegetable garden, and some flower beds for mama were just a few ideas that crossed my mind.

It would have given her something to occupy her time and possibly put a smile on her face. It could've been a house big enough to safely raise children, space for them to spread out and blossom uninhabited by abuse. Instead, He methodically constructed his den of iniquity, piece by mix-matched piece. Much of the construction of the house was made from scrap wood. He only purchased what he couldn't splice together. The house had a crawl space just like daddy's house where certain things were stored. I knew that because my curiosity led another kid and me to a lye tin used to make soap and other things. We got lye all over us. I remember clawing at my skin because it was itching so badly. Mama covered us with some type of heavy grease to ease the itch.

I prayed the house would burn like the piles of trees and brush he burned after clearing the land. I willed it to fall off its blocks and crumble to the ground. I didn't want to live in that house, no matter how big or small my room would be. All the rooms and everyone in them belonged to him. For a time, I believed he owned me too.

My room had a twin bed, a chest with four drawers, and the barest of necessities. I wanted a girly room, a pink chenille bedspread with fringes around the bottom. I wanted a radio or a record player. I wanted a pretty colorful girl's room like I had seen in books or magazines. Our house was amazingly small, considering the land it sat on. There were only two bedrooms, a small living room, and an even smaller kitchen.

He built a perfect four room box. That took considerable ingenuity, he must have stayed up for hours figuring out the floor plan. I don't recall us ever having a dining table. I know we never sat at a table together and had a meal as a family. We had a sofa and a wood-burning stove in the living room, and that's where we ate our food. There was picture window with a view of the dirt road, and that same pasture with the bull Mack enjoyed taunting. He and mama also had a bed and chest in their bedroom, with a baby crib for my baby sister. He promptly accessorized their bedroom with a convex mirror, positioned to monitor the short hallway between our rooms. Careful never to miss an opportunity to witness my startled reaction was foremost on his mind. He made sure I felt uncomfortable at all times.

He taunted me any chance he got, "We got to dig a shit house tomorrow, gal."

I thought to myself, "Shitting in the slop jar is fine with me, considering I was constipated most of the time. A slop jar is a country term for a container used for urinating or defecating when you don't have indoor plumbing. Mama would have to boil water, pour it in a bucket, and have me seal it with my butt. The steam would loosen my bowels to relieve the constipation. It usually worked. I damn sure didn't want any part in building a shithouse.

Building the shithouse was much like digging the well but on a much smaller scale. He didn't dig as deep or as wide, just deep enough to cover his head. It wasn't a several-day job. We were shitting comfortably by nightfall. The shithouse turned out to be the only place for a brief peace of mind. Ours didn't have the fancy crescent moon shape cut into the door. I could have just a few minutes of uninterrupted thoughts in there. Sometimes for several minutes, I'd hide, just peering in the splintery hole where your butt goes, staring at the maggots below swimming in shit. Thinking about my shitty life and how it came to pass.

There's not much entertainment in the country, so you had to be creative. I watched as the maggots seemed to be happier than I. At least they were living as intended, serving their purpose. The toxic ammonia smell didn't bother me one bit. I was accustomed to his awful armpit funk, which was quite similar in my mind. I preferred the company of the maggots. I felt like jumping in on occasion or two. That's how shitty I felt.

A short escape to daydream with my maggot friends was well worth the ass whipping I anticipated. Ignoring his royal summons was a No No. I cherished every moment away from his reach or glaring eyesight. Memories of those years now, five decades later, I still get a hard lump in my throat and weep silently, just as I did back then. I made up nursery rhymes to sing to myself. Actually, I reworded the ones Mack had taught me.

Mama kept herself busy inside the house. She probably was trying to stay out of sight as well. She cooked whatever he killed and skinned. Delectable roadkill entrees, like, squirrels, rabbits, armadillos, even nasty opossums. He skinned a pregnant armadillo once right in front of me while making sickening jokes

44

about the dead baby armadillos. That mama armadillo was dinner that night. He knew I would have a hard time stomaching dinner recalling the tragic chain of events leading to our mouthwatering dinner.

He kept smacking loudly, saying, "Best damn mama armadillo I dun ever ate." Then, glaringly gazing at me for a reaction.

I kept my head down and pretended not to acknowledge his delight in being obnoxious. Like most country folk, we had domestic fowl. We had chickens, a rooster, and a few guineas. That meant again, we had to construct a chicken coup so that the chickens could have a nice peaceful home to nest and lay eggs. They were being fattened up for the kill. Soon there would come a time to wring the chicken's neck, chop its head off, dip it in boiling water, pluck the feathers off, and then singe it over the fire to get any last feathers off. In short order, barnyard fried chicken was served for dinner. There were many reasons that I had developed a poor appetite; meal prep was number one.

Waking to the sound of the rooster crowing on a school day was a private joy unless He decided that I should stay home for some odd reason. Like, putting a glass of water on the porch, retrieving it after a few minutes, and loudly declaring, "The water is frozen. It's too cold for the gal to go to school."

Joy faded, it abruptly turned into an unpredictable day with the tyrant. He had planned to stay home from work, which was the reason for pretending to care that I might get frostbitten going to school.

My safety and comfort were always farthest from his mind. He had a trick up his sleeve, and all roads led to torturing me in some form or fashion. Some days he would just have me shadow him all day long, walking for miles through the woods. He might not even speak too much along the way. He almost seemed normal. But that was all part of his manipulation and control.

He and he only held the emotion keys. He set the tone every minute. Our brief happiness or normalcy was at his discretion. He could go from sitting down helping me draw something for school (he was an amazing artist) to grabbing a handful of my privates as he passed. Seeing me jump and cover myself tickled him to no end.

One day I overheard mama reading a letter to him. He said, "Read that again."

I almost blew my cover when I realized he could not read. I finally found something relating to him extremely funny. I ran out to the outhouse to have a belly-aching laugh. I knew something about him that he didn't know I knew. I knew that he couldn't read. I chuckled and took a nice shit in his dumbass honor. I immediately came up with a way to talk to mama without his interception. I thought of writing notes to communicate behind his back.

I was more ready to start school than ever. Knowing he was dumb as a box of rocks inspired me to read everything I got my hands on. I wanted to be nothing at all like him. I would do exactly as I had promised Mack. I would do well in school. Around this time, I was old enough to grasp the full spectrum of what was happening to me. My spirit had begun to break. I walked around every day with a lump in my throat and belly full of butterflies. He made sure I felt lousy and uncared for.

The first note I gave mama was a plea to take me away. I know that because that was the gist of all the notes I passed. Every one of them was a plea to leave, to go anywhere, just away from him because he was hurting me. I wanted the pain to stop. Mama always responded with a nod, keeping her eyes away from mine. Knowing she had no means of supporting herself and was just as helpless as I was. Mama was simply a poor southern woman trapped in an abusive marriage, obeying her husband's commands as she had vowed to through thick and thin.

Never once did she permit herself to have a say in her own life. Standing up to him was something she just didn't know how to do. Kicking his ass out, calling the police, or bringing him close to meeting his maker for molesting her daughter was not in her either.

Daddy had taken a blind eye to the situation after his prophecy materialized. He allowed the first grandchild to fend for herself, all while knowing mama had mental health issues. Not once did he nor anyone come to my defense.

I fully understand why they all lied by omission. If any of mama's siblings, including Mack, had informed me of mama's condition, they would have felt obligated to stay around to check on us. For them, I believe it was a huge relief to be free, to live their own lives away from the confines of Bullard and Daddy's vile tongue. I wanted the same. Therefore I understand them looking for greener pastures, but what about "No child left behind." The last two to leave had a double wedding if that puts greener pastures in the proper perspective.

Our newly built house was covered with black felt roofing paper. It was fastened to the house with shiny square nails called roofing nails. Maybe we had them on the roof also. The black felt is like a wrapper before the sturdy exterior siding is applied. The house remained dressed in black, with big flat silver buttons. It faded into the night skylight as if the stars had come down from the sky.

Keeping the house black was another form of his calculated oppression. Making us feel depressed by providing a gloomy, negative home life. It was a clever way to bring our moods down through color and texture association. Bad and ugly things are referred to as dark or black. He was conditioning us to settle into a dark off-the-grid lifestyle. He planned to dim my light and make every day and night darkness.

My home displays the flower child in me. From the moment you enter my doorway, splashes of vivid color and greenery greet you. Green is my favorite color, so various green hues are throughout my home. I love yard sales and thrift stores, so I probably have too much of something, but I love my mix of old and new. I have a Yorkie named Zorro. He's very demanding, but he keeps me company and agrees with everything I say. I also have a family of fancy goldfish that intermittently fasts when I forget to feed them.

My bathroom is a sanctuary, inside my sanctuary, where I spend a lot of time soaking in the tub dreaming up my next adventure. A woman's home should feel welcoming and cozy. It should reflect her personality in some way. I enjoy peace and quiet as well as loud music. I love to cook, enjoying the aroma of the goods I've prepared. I love long walks in the park and dinners alone or with a companion, making me realize, more than ever, there were many aspects of Mama's life she had no say in.

Mama may have wanted some of the same simple luxuries, to decorate her own home however she saw fit, highlighting her favorite colors. What kinds of flowers would she have planted in her garden? Would she have shopped for household accessories, like a bedspread with matching curtains, if given the opportunity? Would she dress the walls with artwork or hang family photos? Did she even care that the walls were checkered with mix-matched boards that could have at least been covered with cheap wallpaper?

The only thing that hung on the living room wall was their marriage license, the only indication a female resided in the home. He often pointed to it as he declared, "I'm the damn boss here, and don't forget it. This is my motherfucking house." I thought to myself, "He sure is proud of this ugly ass house." Thank God He was not privy to my thoughts. I was very good at looking down. I tried my best not to look directly at him or give him the satisfaction of seeing how sad I felt inside. I would not make eye contact. It was the only control I had. No matter how hard he tried, he could not control my eyes and thoughts. I could redirect my mind, and I could close my eyes whenever I wanted.

Forced to experience feelings I was too young to compartmentalize appropriately led to many sleepless nights. I would lie awake crying and begging for God to end my life. Every night I said my prayers, not like Mack taught me, "If I die before I wake, I pray to the Lord, my soul will take."

Instead, I recited, "I hope to die before I wake; I pray to the Lord my soul will take, Amen." But every morning, the Lord woke me up despite my sincerity. Thankfully it takes quite a long time to will yourself dead through prayer.

The first day of school finally came. I had survived to see the fourth grade. I felt so old and tired but glad to hear the bus engine grind to a stop in front of our house. The house being black was furthest from my mind until I boarded the bus, and some kid yelled, "Look at her spooky black house."

After that, all the kids started chiming in and making fun of our house. I was so embarrassed that I quickly found a seat and buried my head in my chest until we got to school. When the school bus screeched to a halt at the front of the school, I breathed a sigh of relief.

Half smirking, I thought to myself, "He cannot touch me at school." The school was everything to me. Learning came easy because of my eagerness to absorb information. On the other hand, he couldn't read, spoke incorrectly, and couldn't spell any of the curse words he called mama and me. Being opposite of what he represented was my driving force. I read everything I got my hands on. I was most captivated by the dictionary. The proper enunciation of words fascinated me.

Every time he threatened us or barked some type of foul sentiment in his backwoods dialect, I swiftly corrected his words in my head, and directed pleasantries right back at him. Constantly I reminded myself, I was more brilliant than he would ever be. Mack's encouraging words, "Do good in school Lee," was my driving force.

After a while, the kids on the bus stopped teasing me about my black house. It was an eyesore for sure that was waiting for me every day after school. Maybe the kids eventually noticed how slowly and sadly I exited the bus and perhaps felt sorry for me. My legs felt like they weighed a ton. I literally dragged myself off the bus.

Walking inside as slowly as possible without coming to a complete stop, praying each time I would die before I stepped onto the porch. At nighttime, the house was almost invisible. It blended into the dark country skyline, making it much eerier. I rarely was able to sleep uninterrupted. While most other children slept peacefully, I could not. He came like a thief in the night to steal my innocence again and again. He would usually wait until he knew I had fallen asleep.

Awakening to his hands fumbling around inside my underwear was common. Instantaneously my heart thumped in my ears. Pushing him away and crying only intensified his advances. There was no way I could out-power him. So I stopped fighting and made my body as board-like as possible. I pressed my hands firmly against my eyes until I could only see red while waiting for it to be over again.

Over time I was able to guesstimate how long each session of torture would last. Minutes felt like hours because once he was done torturing me, I, of course, couldn't fall asleep right away. It took a while for my adrenaline glands to get the message he had slithered back into the hole from which he came.

I silently sang the nursery rhyme *London Bridges Is Falling Down*, changing the wording to, "*This old house is falling down--lock him up, lock him up!*" By the time I got to my last, "*My Fair l-a-d-y,*" he would stop abruptly and walk away, leaving his foul odor on my skin. His hands always felt dry and dirty, with a metallic scent. I loathed the way he left me smelling like him. I wanted to be skinned like I had seen him skin a rabbit for dinner. I wanted my own skin removed. I felt the grime from his body embed into mine. The entire house reeked of his grossness.

Thankfully, whatever he did to himself, he didn't force me to see. My eyes always stayed tightly closed but drowning out his heavy breathing was hardest. I couldn't put my finger in my ears. If only I had enough hands to cover myself and fight simultaneously. I had developed my own private dark side to cope with my reality. I became pretty clever at rearranging songs to fit the annoyance. I had learned to adapt the best I could, to stay sane. I learned to grit my teeth and bear it until the end of the song.

He never forced me to touch him or perform any sexual act on him. I was only about fifty pounds soaking wet. He must have seen something in my little eyes that suggested I might do damage. Dynamite comes in small packages. I always tried to fight him off, so he was wise to keep his appendage hidden. I am forever grateful for his grace. In that instance alone, I can vouch for his restraint, for lack of a better word. After all, he is human.

There's a phrase common in the Black community, "God puts no more on you than you can bear." A child should not have to endure such disgusting experiences. Living in a black house with a violent child predator and a severely depressed, detached mother was teetering on the unbearable.

I had to "root hog or die," country way of saying, fight to survive, or give up and die. The fighter in me chose to root hog, forcefully, like a pig without a ring in his nose. Slowly but surely rooting out of that big black pigpen. I wanted to come out of the darkness into a bright shiny new life. That was an ongoing dream.

I recently saw a kid wearing a shirt with the phrase, "Don't stop your daydream." It made me think about all the daydreaming I did as a kid to offset my harsh reality. Something as subtle as a phrase on a shirt of a nine-year-old can spiral into a whole dialogue in my head. An insignificant mental entanglement like that is only one example of the long-term effects of childhood trauma.

There are countless triggers intricately embedded into my being. I accept I am forever affected, but I am in a safe place now. I have transformed that negativity from my past into a strong connectedness with my own children and grands. Love is an action, and my actions have shown an abundance of love to them all.

GAWKER

Mirror mirror on the wall
Who's the scariest of them all?
The evil one that hung you there.
Catching my reflection, clothed or bare.
Used to taunt and humiliate,
You never make me feel great.
Mirror, mirror on the wall.
I am waiting for the day you fall,
shatter yourself into a million pieces,
once and for all...

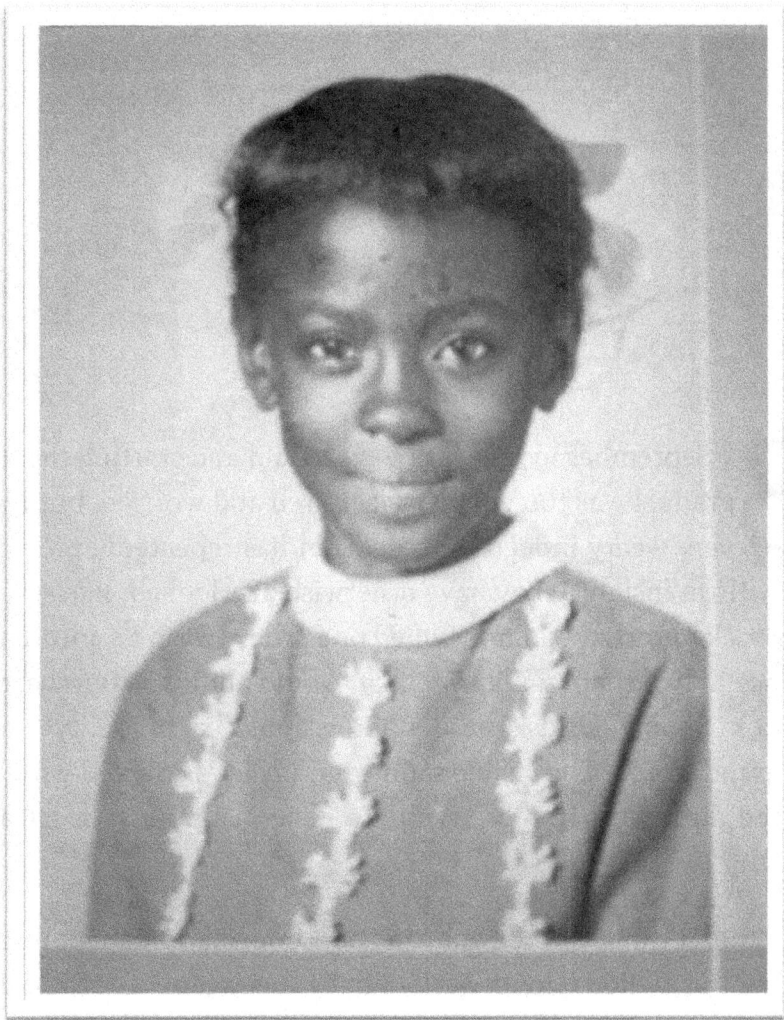

CHAPTER 5

1+2=3

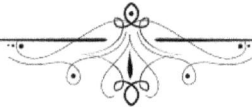

B y September 1971, I was ten years old and starting the fifth grade. I was too young to feel tired and worried, but I was very weary indeed. Ancesty.*com* has repeatedly provided me with an insight I may have otherwise overlooked, like several yearbook photos. I had not owned one. There wasn't a snowball's chance in hell that an illiterate man would allow the purchase of a book of any kind. These photographs, each loudly say a thousand words. The visible sadness in my eyes coupled with my pursed lips, desperately trying to fake happiness, is clearly evident.

I didn't think I would gain any new information about myself during this tedious investigation, but I was wrong. Each chapter has brought new ideas and perceptions I never imagined. Examining each photo is like opening a time capsule filled with buried whimpers and screams. Seeing myself with evidence of lack of sleep, a visible lack of expression, marked by the forced smile on my face, reveals a worried and heavily burdened kid. The camera lens captured what was ignored for so many years.

It prompted me to cover the left side of the photos with my thumb. To me, it appears the right side of my face had a glimmer of happiness. On the left, not so much. However, that glimmer was nothing more than God's grace and mercy, preventing me from losing all hope. The cameraman always encouraged me, "Come on, smile, big, pretty girl." *Smile for what?* I thought. Hiding years of hurt behind the cutest white high collared blue dress, with three rows of tiny, embroidered daisies on the chest, how innocent I should have been, but wasn't thanks to him.

I had to worry about my safety, and at the same time, I was in a constant state of nervous apprehension that no one seemed to notice. It was turning out just as he had planned, instilling fear and hopelessness. I was shaken, scared, and worn down. When the sun went down, I would immediately begin to shiver. God forbid it was a stormy night with crashing thunder and lightning flashing in the window to add a more chilling effect. Shadows from the holes in the window shade took on all kinds of weird formations in my imagination. With covers over my head, shaking, my heart pounding, and fingers clenching my scratchy blanket, many nights, I would rock myself to sleep.

Every morning I was eager to get dressed and leave for school. I wanted to get on the bus without any interaction with him at all. I yearned for a day starting without anxiety or being startled. I prayed he would leave for work without his usual parting announcement, "I'll be home 'fore dark."

On one such morning, while hurriedly getting dressed, I felt his presence. I turned around, sure enough, there he was, peeping through my window. He burst out laughing, grabbing at his stomach as if he had heard the funniest joke ever. I was about fifty pounds, skinny and frail, still he was aroused by my underdeveloped body.

After that, mama tried to hide me. She said to get dressed in the kitchen. There was a small space between the stove and the cabinets. "Put your clothes on right here," gesturing at the small area beside the stove. There was only one window in the kitchen and it faced a wall. From that angle, he couldn't see me. There was just enough space to fit in and get dressed for school. Mama had to feel torn, constantly thinking ahead to what he might do to me next. I used our secret dressing area a few times before he figured out why he could no longer view me from the window.

Foiling our plans, he cleverly drilled two peepholes in my bedroom wall and covered it with a calendar. Accidentally knocking the calendar off the wall, I saw two holes spaced apart where two eyes could fit, causing me to lose my balance. Peering through those peepholes, I began to shiver. I could see that they were directly across from our hiding place. He had continued to watch me with that winning smirk on his face. I felt so defeated, so small, and so trapped. Head in my hands, I sat on the floor trembling. He was always one step ahead spying on us, relishing in our failed attempts to outsmart him.

Voyeurism involves becoming sexually aroused by watching an unsuspecting person who is disrobing, naked, or engaged in sexual activity. Voyeurs do not seek sexual contact with the people being observed. Voyeurism usually begins during adolescence or early adulthood.

In a not-so-roundabout way, he let us know he would do whatever he wanted, whenever he wanted, and we had better get accustomed to his way of life. This chapter, for me, has been the hardest to write, revisit, and relive. I have procrastinated on completing it not from writer's block but from anxiety. My fingertips leave sweat stains on the keyboard. I have a heaviness in my chest and a lump in my throat. That day is as clear as if it were yesterday.

"You are going to help so many people by empowering them to tell their stories. I am proud of you. Keep going!" I am motivated and encouraged by those words from my friends and family.

Otherwise, I would save myself this self-prescribed agony. Childhood trauma is repeated every day across this world. Millions of children out there, as I type, are experiencing far worse than I live to tell. My story is unique only to myself, and I am not naive to believe it will change the world and stop child victimization. Though, I am encouraged my story gives a voice to the voiceless.

His odor had the ability to render me catatonic. The stench radiating off his body was repulsive, the most sickening smell produced by any human. He smelled like something rotting. I knew he was near me before I saw him, before those grimy hands even touched me. I think he enjoyed his disgusting odor. It suited him perfectly, like the animal he is, leaving his scent on everything he touched, securing his territory with a barrier of funk. The proper term is alienation.

Head down, fingers tucked under her pregnant belly, mama sat on the bed, despairingly looking at the floor. She was pretending to ignore my protest. My heart began to pound right out of my chest, and I felt my skinny legs start to tremble. Right away, I felt something awful was about to happen to me. I felt faint. I knew being called to their bedroom was trouble. If only it could have been a normal childhood where you get called for punishment or a spanking. I would have been glad to get a beating. I had just gotten home from a weekend visit at Uncle Jana's. I had fun being a normal silly kid with my cousins for a couple of days.

They had begged him to let me go home with them. Jana had four kids. They all had pressured him and Mama, jumping up and down begging, "Please let Lee come, please!" He agreed. This was probably the third time he had allowed me to go with them; unknowingly, it would be my last. He said, "Hope ya' had fun wit'cha lil' cousins. I betcha you was running yo' mouth. I betcha ain't nobody coming get yo' ass less I say so. Git in here now!"

I hadn't said a word. I knew better. What the hell was he talking about? I loved going to Jana's. They always had a feast of food that they ate three times a day. Their house was filled with the smell of food cooking, unlike mine, musty and lacking. I played, watched tv, and relished the opportunity to be a kid. There was no way I would ruin it by talking about "what stays at home." Besides, I didn't believe telling would change my circumstances. Now I know he was just picking a fight to justify his actions against me somehow.

Eyes widening, I heard my heartbeat thrashing loudly in my ears. An odd aura filled the room. It was a different kind of scary feeling in the air. I expected he would make me pay in some way for any joy he perceived me having at Jana's. I thought he would make me do some kind of unnecessary chore. I froze at the doorway and refused to walk into the room. He grabbed a handful of my shirt and sailed my petite frame like a kite onto their bed.

The bed sheets were stained and wreaked of his foul body odor. I curled my body into a ball, wrapped my arms around my legs, and tucked them firmly against my chest. He openhandedly struck me so hard on my butt I saw stars, but I held my composure. I could feel mama touching me, trying to unfold me from the fetal position. The room was spinning. Their voices sounded muffled. I was scared out of my wits.

I heard him directing my little sisters to stay in the living room. "Don't come in hea, imma beat ya' ass," he scolded. They were very small but knew not to cross him. Their tender ears were attuned to my screams and desperate pleas. Until now, I hadn't considered what they witnessed or experienced at an even younger age than myself.

He jutted his chin in my direction. "Take them pants off and sit up by your mama. Don't make me take'em off!"

Mama repositioned herself slightly but continued to look down. Quivering, trying to find my voice, I muttered, "Mama, what is y'all fixin' to do to me?" Neither of them responded. It was as if they were carrying out a plan they had made amongst themselves.

Through tear-stained eyes, I searched mama's face for a glimpse of compassion for me. Stone-faced, she looked down and away. Her appearance spoke volumes. Her clothing choice was mixed and matched, simply worn to cover her body. Her hair was matted to her head. She had not combed it for days. He had taken away every ounce of self-love and any femininity she possessed.

Mama calmly said, "Just do what he say. It will be over soon. I'm not leaving you." Her breath was harsh, and her tongue was parched, making it hard for her to speak clearly. I screamed, "What is he gonna do to me? Please, mama, please make him stop!"

She had no more fight in her; she was tired. Mama had mentally left me long before that day. I could see it in her face and her posture. He had overpowered her in every way. I could cry a river. Whatever was about to happen would. Hell, over a five-year period, I had cried an ocean of tears. Not once did it stop him from hurting me. Finally, I began hysterically screaming, "No, no, stop, please stop. I didn't say nothing to Jana. Please Stop!"

The only thing that kept me from having a cardiac arrest was my age. I felt it thumping under the only clothing covering my frail body.

They both held me firmly on the bed rhythmically they began removing my pants. I tried twisting my legs around each other, but bones don't twist. I was physically not capable of fighting them off for long. The sheer fact of mama helping him drained any strength I had.

After that, everything started moving in slow motion. He had violated me in many ways, numerous times, but mama had not physically assisted him. After hiding me in the kitchen, to now, literally holding me open, for him, broke me down tremendously. I had to take my mind farther away than ever, but my body had to stay with them... I prayed for death at that moment.

I held my breath as long as I could. I was delirious with anxiety. My eyes welled with tears. Silently, repeatedly, I begged God for death. I tried to detach myself with all I had in me, but mama was with him this time. Helping. Not one melody, nursery rhyme, or a place far away came to mind. Mama sat quietly to my left. Her right hand and forearm were holding my left leg. He was on the right doing the same. My legs quivered with fear underneath their firm grasps. I pressed my fingers against my eyes until I could no longer stand the pressure.

He grunted, "Hold ha still." He yanked my right leg open. He then began cramming his gnarly fingers inside me, deeper and deeper. It felt like he was trying to remove my soul. The goal was to ruin any chances of me having a vital reproductive system or making me a sexually unfit adult. But realistically, I'm giving him too much credit. Self-gratification is the only thought that crosses his mind.

Breathing heavily above my head, he growled, "I feed yo' ass, and yo' crazy mammy. I run this shit." I felt mama nervously reposition herself when he spoke so cruelly of her, as she sat there helping him destroy me. I became so rigid that my bones hurt. I think I was trying to break myself in half.

I had strained and stiffened my body and begged for God to take me away. I wanted to die. My skin even felt unfamiliar. Every cell in my body was on high frequency. I wanted to claw myself in utter frustration, but my hands couldn't leave my face. Straining forcefully, I tried to push him out of me. I tried desperately to shit on them; I pissed on them instead.

It was like mama never saw or felt the wetness. They simultaneously loosened their grip, the planned threesome with a child thwarted by an unexpected dousing of my warm piss. I saw my pants and panties in a heap on the floor; somehow, I found strength in my legs to walk. I grabbed them, my hand was shakily headed for the doorway. Glancing at mama in disbelief, I faintly heard her finally speak. She raised her head groggily and spoke directly to him, too ashamed to look at my face and address my agony.

In a monotone whisper, Mama uttered, "I saw you getting your jollies." Looking intently into his eyes for an explanation for his deceit. She had captured the moment of his arousal while ignoring that I was near rigor mortis. Her attention focused on him and purposefully away from me. That day I was taught to trust no one, not even my own mama. I began to develop an intense hatred for them both. He chuckled, "Nah, I was just getting the gal ready to be a good wife ta somebody. You ain't teachin' ha shit, is you?"

Go yo' pissy ass to bed!" He yelled as he pushed the back of my head, causing me to lose my balance and scrape my arm on the splintery door trim. The minor scrape on my arm was no comparison to the tear in my heart. Humiliation is the first emotion that comes to mind, but I have felt a plethora of feelings from that moment on. Gritting his teeth, coldly ordered to mama, "Clean that piss up and fix me something to eat!" Mama went past our room into the kitchen. She came to my room with a cold, wet towel and handed it to me without saying a word. She looked like I felt—trashed. She turned coldly, avoiding eye contact, and went to do as he had instructed.

What did "jollies" mean? I was sickened by it all. Jollies and ready to be a wife, what was this? I did not want to find out. I sure did not want to be anything like a wife or mother if it meant doing these horrible things to my children. Wreaking of all our body odors, his disgusting stench engulfed me as I consoled myself. I had to fall asleep smelling and feeling like garbage.

I must have cried for hours. Mama never came back to check on me. I'm sure he wouldn't allow it because it was all a part of the control he had over us both. He was destroying her motherly instincts little by little. That night like many previous, he made loud sex noises, apparently wanting all of us to hear them having sex. He thrives on vulgarity and disrespect of the family unit. There was no way she wanted sex with him after what he had just done to me with her help. He had made her an accomplice to his indecency, making it less likely she would seek help. Or was it simply another way of destroying her already fragile self-esteem? That had to be one of the lowest points of her life; torn and afraid.

I'm sure he leveled all sorts of threats against her. The humiliation and guilt of that day alone surely riddled her with tremendous anxiety. What could he have possibly told her to convince her to help him hurt me in that way? Did she really believe they were teaching me a valuable life skill? His pungent odor lingered throughout the house for hours. Lying in bed, still shivering, with my stomach-churning still trying to process what had happened. The house had a thick, musky, dank smell. That day it seemed more unappealing than ever. How could they?

I was so wounded and confused. Over and over again, his words replayed in my head, "Getting me ready to be a good wife." For who exactly? How was what they did to me, a ten-year-old, preparation for marriage? I had experienced a lot, enough to know I had to fight harder somehow. A considerable part of my character was taken away that day, shattered and blown away, like a daffodil, destroyed in an instant by one foul breath.

The next day, it was as if nothing ever happened, mama didn't speak about it, and I wanted to forget. If it were that easy, I would have nothing to write about. I would erase every humiliation from my memory bank. The "threesome" will be the first cancellation. Years ago, I was asked if I had engaged in a threesome. I replied, "Hell naw," but immediately remembered that horrible evening. I have not shared that encounter until now.

Repeatedly he degraded and downgraded any existence. My true identity was gradually stolen as parts of his twisted way of life leached into mine, affecting my every thought. How could I not be changed? I'd been reprogrammed from repetitive mind-altering situations. It changed me from a happy-go-lucky child into a womanly girl in emotional turmoil. I had to find a way to peace. I had to find my voice, and I had to find a way out, with or without mama's help.

I wanted to be nothing like mama or him. I viewed mama as timid and weak, someone afraid to protect her own children. I viewed him as a dumb, evil man. I grew stronger, smarter, and more intuitive from their poor qualities. I began to mimic mama's nonchalant attitude. My replies were with a flat affect, I rarely started up a conversation. Instead, I occupied my mind with school, songs, poetry, daydreaming, and saying curse words. My secret lingo was filled with f-bombs. It is no longer a secret.

Nothing, and no one came to our house unless he agreed, and we never left to go anywhere without his approval first. My understanding of religion, speaking in tongues, laying hands on folks, and prayer was confusing. Religion appeared wishy-washy. We didn't bless our food. The Lord's Prayer was taught to me by Mack. When she moved away, I toyed with the wording to suit my needs, not knowing that God had my back all along. Except for weddings, I had not been to a church in years. He was not a "God-fearing" man. In his house, he served himself. He wanted to possess our minds, bodies, and soul.

There was a popular preacher who slapped people on their foreheads, knocking them to the ground. They claimed they were healed of whatever ailment they were burdened with when they stood up. The preacher was a white man named Reverend A.A. Allen, who had a tv show. White folks lined up waiting to get knocked out by his mighty healing hand. It fascinated me, and because it was on tv, I believed it to be true. I didn't understand religion. How God played a role in our lives was unrecognizable to me at the time. Sometimes you can't see the forest for the trees.

The Devil himself ruled with an iron hand at our house. If only Reverend A. A. Allen could have slapped the hell out of him, literally, because he is definitely a hellion. For some odd reason, he trusted Jehovah's witnesses to come to the house for bible study regularly. Naturally, he did not take part. He had probably instructed mama to pray on his behalf, to atone for his despicable sins. Perhaps he feared trusting us to go to church where the pastor might be just like him. More so, maybe Mama might reach out for help from one of the church ladies.

He could monitor us better at home. I sure hope he didn't count on having a bible in the house to save him from purgatory somehow. Nor did it save me from the hell he put me through from one Sunday 'til the next. Jehovah's Witnesses do not observe holidays, such as Christmas, Easter, and birthdays. They do not salute the flag or sing the national anthem. They also refuse to join the military. The only thing he got from their teaching was the denial of children's participation in anything joy-filled; that bit of information appealed to his narcissism. Denying his own children of anything to smile about bolsters his lack of empathy

Did our devil sing and celebrate? Sure he did. He treats every day as a holiday. He rejoices and laughs loudly as he ruins the day for his own family. He admonishes himself with every guiltless pleasure his cold heart desires. For whatever self-serving reason, he wanted us to be Jehovah's Witnesses. We were learning the books of the bible inside the devil's lair.

Looking back, it was a very cult-like lifestyle. We had the pleasure of going to The Kingdom Hall for services a few times with one of his cousin's wives. For me, it was a few hours to relax, inhale the fresh air, and daydream. The calming voice of the speaker helped my mind travel.

It was my time to calm myself, a rest stop, so to speak. I could have cared less about the religious messages. I imagined going somewhere with Mack and never coming back. I thought about us playing "patty cake" or reading a book together and acting silly. I strongly believe in the power of prayer, visualizations, and/or journaling your wants and needs. Put them in the atmosphere, and then wait for them to manifest. Still, some action is required at the same time—all forces, spiritual and physical, working together make dreams and prayers become manifestations.

I habitually recited my own fragmented versions of the Lord's Prayer silently throughout the day. I did what I could to take some sense of control over my destiny. I was desperately trying to stay mentally afloat by all means necessary. The Lord's Prayer boggled me. Its meaning, like everything else, was not explained. Prayer and religious music were taught in school, but their meaning was not. We sang the songs and prayed without inquiry. Children did not ask questions; they obeyed.

Was "messing with me" God's will? If not, why was it happening? I was confused about God's will. Why wouldn't God, or Jehovah, do something good for Mama and her children? Why did God put such an evil person in our lives? The billion-dollar question is, "How can we remove people that hurt children from society?" Then, I found this article online by legal analyst Robin Sax:

The law identifies certain people as mandated reporters: psychologists, doctors, law enforcement, teachers. Absent from that list are parents. While parents are not on the list as mandated by the law, parents can be accused of, and criminally responsible for, failing to protect their child if they don't call. While there may not be an affirmative duty that a penal code says you have to do, you could find yourself in a situation where you could be held liable or criminally responsible for not taking action in protecting your kids. That's particularly important, not just for the parent who may think that someone sexually abused their kid outside of the home. It becomes a huge game-changer when the perpetrator is inside the home and you are allowing the abuse to continue. A woman lives with her husband's convictions, as if they have been sentenced themselves. They tell themselves that they lacked something. If they had been good wives and partners, why would their men have turned to sex offending? It's an irrational response, but it is based on a deep feeling that the person you thought you knew was a stranger.

READY

Ready to cry,

Ready to die,

Ready to leave,

Ready to believe,

Ready to castrate,

Ready to hate,

Ready to turn to dust

Ready to combust,

Ready to prosper,

Ready for someone to offer,

Ready or not

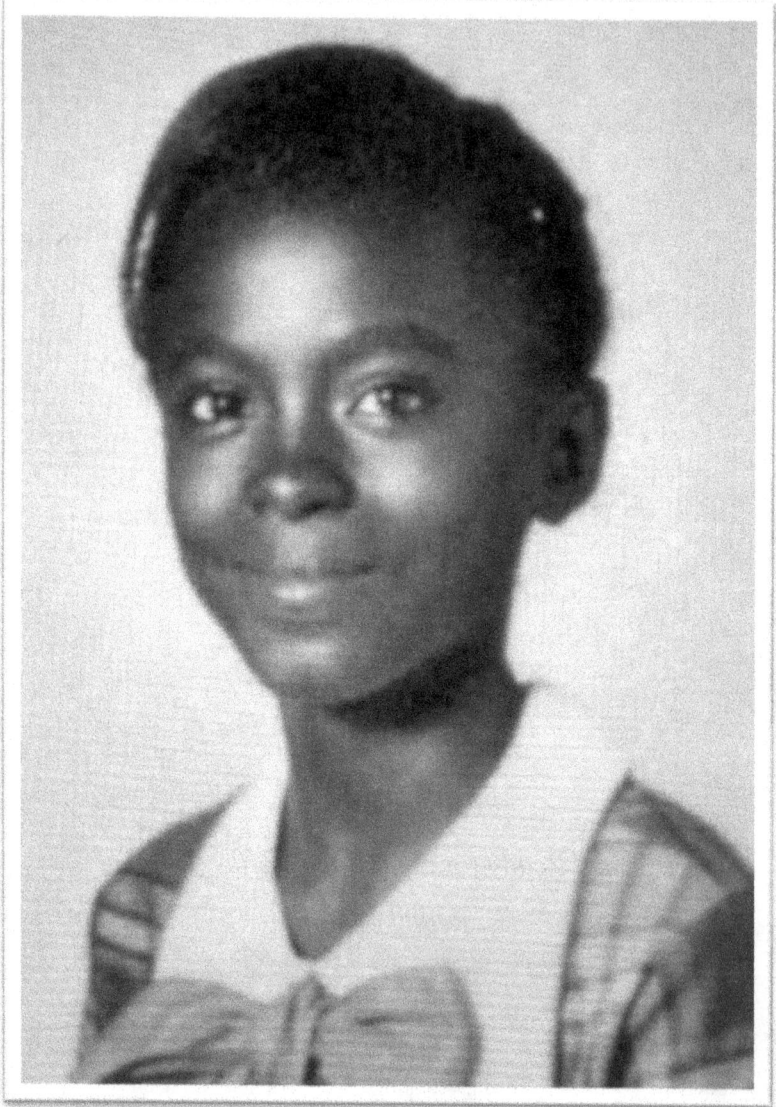

CHAPTER 6

ATTEMPTED RAPE

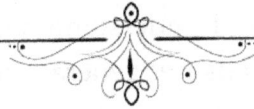

By the time school started again, mama had four children, with one on the way. She had brought three new lives into the world in less than five years of marriage. At only twenty-six years old, she was responsible for the well-being of four helpless children. As a big sister, my role was to be a friend, someone to look up to, and the person giving words of encouragement to my baby sisters and brothers. I needed a big sister for myself. I needed a shoulder to lean on. How could I explain their imminent danger? They were babies, babies that I had not bonded with at all. Besides, they, unlike myself, were born into hell's inferno. They had felt his wrath in the womb from mama's constant state of depression and self-loathing. They had heard me begging and pleading with their daddy to "Stop!" all their lives. They were too young to understand what was happening to me. I surely felt the repercussions emotionally and definitely physically. He laid hands on all living creatures; babies were not spared.

At some point, we all slept together in a twin bed, so it's entirely possible they were startled awake many times by the commotion of me trying to fight him off, wondering what the hell was going on. Their sleep was interrupted as well. Knowing his mode of Operandi (MO), they were sitting ducks. The disservice he proudly provided to his own flesh and blood, and the sheer disregard for giving any of us a fair start in life, is unconscionable. Raising confident, mentally stable children was furthest from his warped mind. He dared not instill great values, such as family support through love and understanding. His callous disregard for the family structure ensures generations of disconnectedness. Moreover, he happily disturbed the natural bonding process, which pains me the most.

About twenty-five years ago, I typed an entire page to The Oprah Winfrey Show explaining my separation from my siblings and how we needed a panel of therapists to help us heal as a unit. I realized I had not sent the email many weeks later, probably because I needed an email address. I laughed at my computer illiteracy and took it as a sign not to let sleeping dogs lie. My computer skills were hilarious then, and still are a bit laughable today.

All jokes aside, I believe a professional family group therapy setting is the only way we can reunite solidly. Group family therapy is one of my dreams I'm willing to share. A single mother struggling alone would have been a much better option for us. Mama's extended family may have been less afraid to step up and mitigate her weaknesses, thereby giving us all a fair chance at normalcy.

The start of a new school year was all I looked forward to.

My fifth-grade teacher was Mrs. Ann. She said, "Say here and raise your hand when I call your name." When she got to mine, I was not paying attention. I heard her raise her voice a few octaves, "Artie Nolen!" I jumped and sat up straight, hand raised, "Here I am, ma'am." Mrs. Ann dismissively said, "Oh, I was expecting a boy." The kids laughed and joked about my 'boy' name. Being teased was uncomfortable, but I had developed a thick skin no child could penetrate. I let their silliness roll off me, like water off a duck's back.

I took a special interest in the dictionary. I had a lot of words that needed defining. Each student was assigned a book for the year for each class. I loved writing my name in the space provided at the front of the book. In those days, the books were returned at the end of the year, and they had better be in good condition. I recall the awkward paper book covers with the thick envelope glue on the corners; so that the cover fits snugly. They helped keep the books nice for the next student.

I scanned the dictionary for new words I had heard over the summer and wrote down any new ones that caught my eye. There was something about learning to enunciate words correctly, and thereby increasing my vocabulary was something meaningful to focus on. Then, after learning the proper way to write a letter, I wrote to Mack as often as possible. Finding this letter I wrote to her nearly fifty years ago speaks to our solid bond.

Knowing he couldn't read a lick consciously propelled my academic wanting. Jollies was the first word I looked up. That word had haunted me since that horrible day when I first heard it come from mama's mouth. I wanted to know what mama was disturbed by. What was the action that brought her to life at that moment? Webster's dictionary's meaning in 1972 did an injustice to the implication mama was referring to, though he indeed was overjoyed, and quite amused.

Today, the urban dictionary provides a more to-the-point

definition of jollies; long story short; he had had an orgasm. Realize may be an overused word in this memoir, but I have come to comprehend so much more about the circumstances leading up to that total lapse in judgment as a mother. I believe that they, at some time, had agreed upon the rules for "getting me ready." He was only to prepare me somehow for a husband. I don't get how trying to destroy my reproductive system at eleven years old would make me a benefactor.

Obviously, he wasn't supposed to get aroused. It was just another trick he had up his sleeve. That lets me know mama was not at all dealing with a full deck. He used mama's mental illness to manipulate her into believing almost anything. As much as she slept at times, he may have kept her drugged. Toying with our minds delighted him. There was nothing too distasteful for his character.

At school, we were taught manners and how to act accordingly, say please and thank you, and not lie, cheat, steal, or fight with each other. My home life was a big fat lie. We weren't a family. We didn't hug and love each other. We didn't address each other with kind words. We merely existed alongside one another. There were no "I'm sorry's," or "please forgive me's" at our home. Repeatedly he degraded and downgraded our existences. His opinion was the only one that mattered. Our intelligence would be limited if it was only his knowledge we received.

My homeschooling was quite the opposite. I was taught that women should do whatever their husbands told them. I was taught to trust no one, including my own mama. I was taught my private parts are not private at all, nor are they mine. I was taught to deceive by feigning normalcy, I followed the rule, what happened at home was nobody's business.

First and foremost, I learned that adults sometimes violate and torture children under the guise of parenting, and if you tell, it only gets worse. I learned to pretend everything is everything, "I'm fine, and you?"

Proverbs 22:6 states, "Train up a child in the way he should go; and when he is old, he will not depart from it."

I trained myself to be strong and speak truth to myself. I taught myself to grit my teeth and just live another day. Suffocating in a bucket like those pitiful baby mice was not an option for me. He and mama inadvertently taught me to fight like hell to survive. The notes I passed to mama became more detailed and disrespectful. I told her she was a bad mama, and I hated them. I wrote, "I am telling Mack what y'all did to me."

Mama looked stunned but did not respond. Mack was far away, and I was afraid he might hurt her. I only wrote it trying to get a reaction from mama. A cold prickly is better than a warm nothing. I was demanding her attention. He had me convinced anyone crossing him would end up hurt badly. Considering no one was rescuing us, I believed him.

When she did speak, Mama's response was short and to the point. She wasn't at all talkative or long-winded. Whatever the conversation, she offered the short to-the-point version—no enthusiasm or excitement in her presentation, not jovial at all, ever. Just when I was trying to reorganize my thoughts, my first menstrual cycle made its debut. After cleaning the chair twice, it took me a moment to conclude that the red stain on the chair was coming from my body. He was not home. I ran frantically to mama. I showed her the blood in my panties.

"Your period started. It will come down every month, at about the same time. She gave me a thick, soft rectangular pad with long pieces on each end. She said, "This is a Kotex." It was much bigger than I had ever needed. She showed me how to fix it in my underwear. She pinned it in place with two safety pins. She handed me a couple and said, "Keep yourself clean down there." It was wide and uncomfortable. I was devastated.

"If your period don't come, that's how you know when you are pregnant." She gave no further instructions or directions. "All women have it every month," Mama nonchalantly explained. "It will last a few days," her words trailed off as she went back to whatever she was doing. She left me with the nightmare of possibly having his babies too someday, soon. Just when I thought things couldn't get any worse.

My knees would ache badly. I didn't associate it with my period that day, but it became an indicator that time of the month was approaching. At school, the girls talked about starting their menstruation in sixth or seventh grade; mine had come early. Mama didn't tell me anything about the "birds and the bees." Being she was "with child" almost every year, she assumed I would figure it all out in due time. I wasn't sure how the reproductive cycle worked, but I knew enough to know he made kids. I was worried and more afraid than ever.

Absolutely nothing got past him. I can imagine mama pleading with him not to pump me full of babies too, and him glowing as she begged. To my delight, he left me alone for those few days. He didn't wash his hands or body very often, so getting blood on his fingers would be too close to the feeling of water, which I think he is afraid of. So I was glad when my knees started to ache; I could expect a reprieve from the nightly cavity check.

Anytime they were having private conversations, I had learned from his sneaky ways to eavesdrop. "I'm the one feeding her lil ass. Ha real daddy don't want ha. I'm ha daddy, change ha name to mine," he demanded.

Mama responded, "I'll see, but you know it won't be free." After hearing it cost money, he yelled, "That's bullshit, it ain't cost shit to give them other chullen my name."

Another lie by omission. No one thought it was my business to know I had a "real daddy" and that he had abandoned me before my birth.

I was stunned. I thought that was why he was so mean and nasty to me. He resented having to provide for another man's child. Now I know, that was simply gaslighting. He is a pedophile, and I was available. Simple facts, it had nothing to do with financial support. The fact my real daddy didn't support me was an asset to him.

I didn't know how to feel, finding out there was a man somewhere that could have come to rescue me, but chose to stay away while I was being tortured. Mama had kept vital information from me. I despised her even more. My heart was pounding. This new revelation stunned me. Daddy was not my daddy. He was my grandpa. Who was or was not my daddy had been the least of my worries. I had to contend with one Daddy (the step).

He asked, "Is she still on the rag?" Mama didn't answer. He yelled, "Is she?" Mama finally responded, "No, she stopped." I figured out that "on the rag" had to do with my period. I felt sick to my stomach hearing them discuss my availability. He yelled. "Cum out here, gal. We going to town." I asked, "For what?" He looked at me and smiled, "Stay in yo' place. You'll see. Come on. I ain't got all day." Mama sat quietly and offered no resistance. I'm sure she had been informed of why we were going to town. He was long past the days of hiding his true intentions.

Every few minutes along the way to town, he would look at me, raising his eyebrows, grinning from ear to ear. He'd reach over and grab between my legs. It never occurred to me to jump out of the truck onto the road. He parked his beat-up old truck at Montgomery Ward's department store in Tyler. I had never been to a department store and surely never expected to go with him. He barked, "Get yo' ass out." The store smelled fresh and clean. All the beautiful colors overwhelmed my senses. For a few moments, I was in awe.

He led me past the girl's clothes, straight to the women's lingerie department. I could only touch some of the pretty dresses as he rushed me past them. Magnificently beautiful colors and textures breezed through my tiny fingers. Was he bringing me to pick out something for mama? I had never seen him give her anything but a hard time. Finally, he picked a garment off the rack. It was white. He looked at me through the sheer fabric, shimmering it from side to side, smiling, teasingly implying the obvious. The trip to town was for me, he was not shopping for mama at all.

81

I made the biggest scene to draw attention. Angrily he grabbed the first thing he could because people started noticing the ruckus. I yelled, "This not the little girls' department. I don't want it!" He punched me so hard I'm sure it left a bruise. He looked at me with his teeth clenched, grabbed me by my arm leading me to the cashier, and paid for the nightgown. The cashier's inquisitive expression revealed she suspected something was wrong but did not dare to interfere. He for sure was going to beat my ass when we got back home.

I was finding my voice and it felt amazing. He cursed and threatened me all the way back home. "You know I'm whoopin' yo' ass when we get home for acting a fool in that sto'." Did his dumbass really think I would cooperate in picking out a provocative garment to help him get a jolly? The ride back home was much faster than going. He had plans for a private fashion show. He was focused on getting back to the house and parading me around in my new adornment. He grabbed the bag jumping out of the truck, almost running inside to show momma what his hard-earned money had purchased.

I slowly dragged myself indoors. "Come on, gal, try it on," he directed. I reluctantly followed him to their bedroom. Being in that room made it hard for me to breathe. He pulled the nightgown out of the bag, draped it over his arms, giving it to mama as if he had purchased the most exquisite garment made. Mama held it up to get a good look. The gown was sleeveless, made of very sheer, soft cotton, and it was baby blue and pink with eyelet trim. "That's pretty," mama dryly said.

"Ain't what I wanted to get. You know that gal acted a damn fool in the sto'. I owe ha' an ass whoopin'. You gone have

82

to fix it." Mama nodded without looking up. It was a small size, but still too big for me. It dragged the floor and hung on my thin body like it was still on the hanger. Mama measured and cut it to his specifications (above the knee) and hemmed it. There is no need to recant another night of dysfunctional sickness. It was the same, except he dressed me for the occasion.

The next few weeks, I pressured mama to do something, anything, to get us all away from him. Knowing he couldn't read, I wrote the notes in all lower-case letters so he couldn't distinguish names from words. Apparently, mama got sloppy with getting rid of the notes. I heard him yelling, "I saw y'all passing your little notes. I got this shit out the trash. What it say, bitch?" Mama started reading the note loudly, but not exactly word for word.

I was listening intently, knowing he was coming for me next. He was yelling and hitting her, saying, "I know that word don't start like that, you lying bitch." He snatched the paper and came into my room. "Get your ass up now. What does it say?" I tried repeating exactly what mama had made up. He had paid attention to what mama said the word was, so when he pointed it out to me, and I didn't say the same word as mama had, he knew we were tricking him. Pushing my forehead, he screamed, "What the fuck it say?!" I refused to answer him. No way I was telling his dumbass anything.

I remember its details because it was the one he found, which set off a firestorm inside him. The note asked where my real daddy was. And I told her I would kill myself if she changed my name to his. I expressed hatred for them both. So there was no way I would read those words to him. It was perfectly fine for him to plot against us, but turning on him was a no-no. He warned, "I got something for y'all smart asses. What y'all cooking up? Ain't nobody fucking with me. This my house! Pray before I kill yo' lil' ass." He pushed me to the floor. "I heard you prayin' that crazy shit. Yo' little ass can die tonight."

I heard mama crying out loud for the first time ever. Hell, all of us were crying. He had awakened the babies with his yelling. "Get on your knees, say the Lord's Prayer out loud so yo' mama can hear your lying ass." He yelled to mama, "Shut the fuck up and get them chullen quiet before I give all y'all sumtin' to cry about." As I began to pray, he came down hard across my back with a belt with every few words.

"Louder!" he yelled. "Keep on passing notes and you gone see. Keep thankin' I'm dumb." He laughed, "How cum I catch y'all every time? Now, who is dumb? Ask the Lord to forgive ya' for thanking you slick." He hit me a few more times and yelled, "Git yo' ass in that bed." We didn't have to "thank." We knew he was dumb as a box of rocks.

He is a functional illiterate that lucked up on the perfect victims. That doesn't make him smart at all, just timely. I was getting smarter every day. My best friend, the dictionary, helped me toy with his mind. I wrote words in cursive in the dirt. Mostly curse words, only to annoy him because I knew that was the one advantage I had on him. He could barely read printed four-letter words, so he damn sure couldn't read cursive. He knew it would be pointless asking me what I was writing.

I lay awake for hours, trying to figure out why he chose the Lord's Prayer to punish me with. It was strange even for him. I didn't even know he knew how to pray. At some point in his life, he may have been normal. However, something terrible happened to him as a child, causing him to act with such cruelty. He was the one needing deliverance, not me. After that night, reciting fragments of the Lord's Prayer in my head throughout the day calmed me. I stopped asking the Lord to let me die in my sleep.

I thought if he was trying to ruin something, it had to be good. So I prayed, "Our Father who art in heaven, please take me away from this place, Amen." Mama and I continued to pass notes, not nearly as often, but we made sure to take them to the outhouse when we did. That outhouse had multiple functions. I would hide there, discard our notes, and talk to my maggot friends. It was a room without a view of me. The outhouse had no windows for him to peer into, no mirror to intimidate. The smell didn't bother me. I was very accustomed to horrible odors, most of which came from him. He had a stench much like the harshness of the outhouse.

I remember it being a scorching day. But, for once, the house was calm. I was doodling on a piece of paper and daydreaming, of course. I heard him tell mama, "I'll be back in a minute. I'm taking Lee with me." It was odd. He rarely called me by name. It was usually gal or yo' ass. "Come on, gal. Let's go." Mama raised her head and nodded with approval as if she had any say in the matter. He wasn't asking for her permission at all. "Where?" I asked with my voice trembling.

I hated being alone with him away from home. Though mama provided little or no protection, I at least had a watchful eye in case he killed me. She appeared in the doorway but knew she had better not interfere. Again, I yelled, "Where are you taking me?"

"*What was he up to this time?*" I thought. He pushed me, "Get in the damn truck! Crying, I called for mama. "Where he taking me now, mama?"

Mama shrugged and never uttered a word. I watched her in the doorway as he slowly drove away. A piece of the floorboard had rotted away in his jalopy of a truck. I focused on the road disappearing underneath my feet. The truck smelled like him mixed with motor oil. I had begun my mental escape. Something was going to happen; it always did. He was going to hurt me. There would be no one to witness the torture I expected would happen. He had that grin on his face that he always displayed just before terrorizing me. I started to feel sick to my stomach. I felt ill most of the time because he ensured I was a nervous wreck.

He pulled the truck off the road and put it in park about a mile or so from the house. He tossed the keys in the air close to my face. He caught them with a snap, taunting me. I knew he was about to get his jollies. An old, abandoned barn was visible from the road, overgrown with tall weeds and grass. It was apparent no one lived there. When he gestured for me to follow him, I nearly collapsed. Seeing that barn in the distance concerned me tremendously. He was grinning and glaring at me. He enjoyed watching me shake and break down.

"Come on, gal. Ain't got all day." He started whistling as he nudged me in the direction of the barn. The barn looked as if a strong wind might blow it down. It felt like I was walking in quicksand. It was a struggle to wade through the tall grass. Luckily, I had on thick corduroy pants. He pushed me the whole way to the barn. Stumbling, crying, and trying not to fall in the

86

tall weeds, we approached the barn entrance with my heart pounding.

The barn was empty for the most part except for the old hay on the ground. Before I could focus on its surroundings, he violently shoved me to the ground. I fell so hard on my butt I thought it was broken. When I fell, he straddled me and started unbuckling his pants. He didn't have any underwear on. I saw his "thang" for the first time. I didn't know the proper term was penis then. He smelled awful. I felt faint. He began trying to rip my pants off. I heard and felt the fabric tearing. Somehow, I was able to twist my body onto my stomach. I dug my toes into the hay, making my body as rigid as possible. My heart was racing. I could hardly catch my breath.

He straddled me, trying to turn me back onto my back. I had gotten eyeglasses recently, and they fell into my hands. I closed my eyes tightly and began twisting them, fearing what was about to happen. That action bought me one more chance at saving myself. He saw the glasses and jumped off me. I ran from that barn as fast as my legs could carry. I tumbled over weeds, tripping over and over again from fear. I was off-balance from running while holding the rip in my pants closed to prevent weeds from getting inside the huge gaping hole. I somehow found myself on the road. I was out of breath, but I kept running. I ran toward the house instead of away. It didn't matter. He would see me on the road.

I did not get very far before I heard the sound of that piece of shit truck eating up the road behind me. The truck stopped abruptly, the dust from the road engine. He grabbed me and threw me in the truck. I was covered with sticker burrs, hay, and anything else I may have collected in my hair and on my clothing. I looked like a miniature scarecrow. I ran into the house hyperventilating. I couldn't get one word to formulate. I tried showing mama my ripped pants, pointing at him as he casually walked in behind me.

"That gal is crazy. She saw a snake, took out running, tore her pants and everythang," he lied as usual. Mama sat motionlessly. She didn't look at me, and she ignored him. Mama just sat there for hours, staring into space. I didn't know it was her illness. How could I? I just knew we needed help! "Crazy girl almost fucked up ha glasses too. I fixed'em," he continued grinning and laughing, telling Mama how scary I was. "Gal scared of her own shadow." Mama continued to ignore the commotion. She didn't even raise her head. What he was doing to me was slowly destroying her.

Mama was emotionally and physically drained, weakened by depression, and demeaned by men she trusted with her love. Mama was mild-mannered by nature, making it easier for her to succumb to his cruelty. The weaker she became, the stronger I knew I had to be. Everyone is familiar with Tyler Perry's character Madea. If you're not, she is a tough, elderly black woman who will open a can of whoop-ass for whoever is so deserving. Mama needed a Madea type in her life to help her make a pot of hot grits to serve her abusive husband. Or someone similarly strong in her corner, guiding and helping her provide a better life for herself and her children.

I realize now that it is quite possible he may not have only intended to rape me. He may have planned to kill me in that barn. I believe he had assured mama digital penetration (fingering) was as far as he would go. Hence, he had to separate us so that mama wouldn't know he had crossed the imaginary line they had drawn. I genuinely believe he was going to stage my accidental death. That's why it was important to him that my eyeglasses were intact. When they found my skeletal remains strewn all over that barn, ripped apart by wild animals, the eyeglasses had to be intact so as not to draw attention. He could make up any story about why he didn't return home with me.

Mama wouldn't go looking for me. She would think I had run away like I had been threatening to do. God, Madea, and all the angels in heaven spared my life and virginity that day. Even if he hadn't killed me, that would have killed my spirit. I don't see how I would have been able to recover. There would not have been an extensive police investigation. The police would close the case; another dead negro child was potentially eliminated. Fast forward ten years, records show he was successful in raping a child. So I am absolutely convinced I dodged several bullets.

The battle was a full-fledged war because he had become bold and upfront with his intentions. He did what he wanted day or night. If I could go back in time and speak to my eleven-year-old self, I would first give her a long overdue, warm, heartfelt, comforting hug. A hug she could trust without the fear of being touched inappropriately. Second, I would encourage her to keep drawing attention to what's being hidden. I would say, "Baby girl, I'm so sorry for all the people who let you down." Third, I would encourage her to keep fighting because God has a plan for her life.

Now I can clearly see how God manifested in my life, time and time again. From day one, his mercy and his grace covered me. All the years before the barn incident, I could have been raped a million times by him. Nothing was stopping him but God. Mama's "fits" and depression could have led her to kill us all and not even remember doing it. So much worse could have happened to me. I thank God for all that did not transpire.

After his failed attempt, I guess he thought it best to switch sides and try to form a pact with me (against myself). He foolishly suggested that if I would not fight back and let him have his way with me, he would let me visit my cousins more often and get this... he promised he would not cheat on Mama with other women. His thought process is warped at best.

I told him, "I don't give a damn what you did or to who you did it to. Just please leave me alone." Sobbing loudly and wiping away a constant flow of tears, I belted out, "I will never stop fighting, and I don't want to go see my cousins anymore anyway." I told him, "I'd rather stay home and not have to cry when they brought me back to our shitty house; and have to think about all the nice stuff they had, and we don't have anything nice because you're a sorry, broke ass, fake daddy!" He punched me hard in the arm and drove us home.

I felt as powerful as the sting in my arm pulsated. I had spoken up, and it felt good. I let him know in no uncertain terms that I didn't give a damn what he deprived me of. There was nothing he could say or do to make me accept his brutality. I cursed a lot whenever I felt like it, aloud or under my breath, the outcome would be the same. I got hit for looking wrong back then. It may as well have been for something worthwhile to me. I had learned from the best. As a matter of fact, cursing felt good.

I had heard Dolomite blaring on Tony's car stereo once

when he stopped by for a short visit. Dolomite was an adult poet with explicit content. Tony was mama's rowdy baby brother. Whenever he stopped by it was always something exciting about his visit. Rarely did anyone come inside our house and chill. It was unwelcoming in every way. I absolutely loved Dolomite. It was rude, offensive, and downright intriguing. Curse words in poetic form. The most taboo words with perfect pronunciation and clarity. "Dolomite is my name, and fuckin' motherfuckas up is my game!" I couldn't believe my ears. I hung on every unsavory word, and I just had to write motherfucker in the dirt in cursive.

By eleven years old, I had been around the block. Or should I say I had been around the barn? I had survived nearly being raped in a barn, or possibly losing my life there. With all that, still fresh on my mind, I didn't hear the teacher call my name during roll call. "Artie, Artie Nolen, is he here?" She shouted. "Here," I said shyly. The teacher inconsiderately stated, "Oh, I was looking for a boy." The kids laughed and started making fun of my "boy name." I couldn't catch a break emotionally. The same experienced repeated again with yet another teacher.

I found the courage to ask Mrs. Hunt to let me go to the office to use the telephone. The secretary let me use the school phone. Of course, she was listening in, not to mention all the country folk nearby were listening in also. Bullard was on a "party line." Anyone nearby could hear my conversation. All you had to do was pick up your phone, and if you heard people talking, the courteous thing to do would be to hang up and not listen. Country folks are nosy by nature, so if someone overheard a child pleading for help, there was no way they wouldn't listen in for the juicy details as they could.

The south was still segregated at some establishments. The laundromat, for instance, had signage boldly printed directing blacks to their less than attractive clothes washing area. So the mere fact a white secretary helped me during those times in itself was nothing short of a miracle. She could have very well refused and sent my black ass back to class. My teacher being white as well, could have refused me permission to go to the office. But, instead, on more than one occasion, they both helped me, try to help myself.

Teachers are amazing people. They provide a layer of protection for children they may never encounter at home. I recall my third-grade teacher providing fresh clothes for a little girl in my class. She even combed her hair so that she blended in with everyone else. That caring spirit stayed with me throughout my life. A teacher's intuition can change the direction of a child's life. I learned early on, all by myself, that there are good and bad people in every race, an important lesson learned for a little Black girl. Nobody came for me, but suddenly he wasn't around either. After a couple of days of thinking my prayers had been answered, that God had taken him away, I asked Mama, "Where is he at?" She, at first, did as usual and ignored my question.

Feeling hopeful and a little too cocky, I yelled, "Is he dead?" Mama said, "Stay in yo' place. When I get hold of you, it's gonna be for the old and the new." She meant it; mama could give some good ass whooping's too. She mostly whooped me for cursing and talking back. Peaceful days and nights without him to torment me felt strange. I was unaccustomed to calm. Not knowing when he might return kept me on edge. Mama kept saying, "Stay out of grown folks' business."

Every action brings a reaction. All the years of abuse had left their mark. Then, one day in the library at school, I was sitting alone at a table, solemnly thinking about one of the many times he "messed with me." All of a sudden, I felt my private area throbbing uncontrollably. Right there in front of God and everybody, that was happening. I had no idea precisely what thought triggered it, but it came over me very unexpectedly.

The librarian was the only Black teacher at the school She had a soft, sweet voice, she was very tall, her perfume made me think about Mack. She had her back to me. I squeezed my legs together to try to make it stop. It intensified the feeling. My heart raced as the warmth engulfed me. I sat there, afraid to move. I thought for a minute I had peed on myself. Embarrassed and ashamed, I raised my head to realize no one noticed. I cried silently as I did at home, swallowing my tears and bearing my grief alone. I understood that experience was related to what he had done to me repeatedly.

I felt dirty. I believed he had made me nasty like him. I hated myself and what he had done to change me. The rest of the day at school, I was in a daze. All I could think about was trying not to let that happen again. But, of course, it did reoccur. His repeated tampering with my developing anatomy caused a knee-jerk reaction at the oddest times. Masturbation in children is one of the brightest red flags in identifying sexual abuse. Stressful situations or changes in routine can often trigger the need for a child to pleasure themselves. Parents must be willing to address this issue rather than deny what they know as unusual behavior, often learned from adults or older children. Unfortunately, he had forced me into a world that I was too young to compartmentalize appropriately, leaving me with adult desires trapped in a child's body.

After a few weeks of him still missing, a car pulled up to the house. It was his Jehovah's Witness cousins' wife. She was alone. I found that very odd. Mama got up and grabbed some bags she had stashed in our temporarily secret dressing area. Mama had kept a secret of her own. She knew exactly where he was all along. Mrs. Lady said, "Y'all ready to head north? It's gonna be a long bus ride to Chicago. Sis, you sho' you want to leave yo' family? You don't know nobody up there." Mama nodded and said, "I got to go, he waitin' on us."

Mama had packed our clothes for the trip. It's not as if we owned a lot. I heard her say she had also made some food for us to take along. I had prayed to go far away, but I meant far away without him. Mrs. Lady drove us to the Greyhound bus station in Tyler. She made sure mama got our tickets, and they said their farewells. I had no way of saying goodbye to Mack or letting her know where we were going. He wanted to make sure nobody talked some sense in mama while he was gone. He had instructed her to alert no one. I was devastated. I thought I would never see Mack again.

Boarding the bus was nothing like the school bus. It was vast and cold inside. Mama scrambled to find a seat for all of us. The bus driver pulled the door closed and announced several stops before we arrived in Chicago in two days. The move was overwhelmingly abrupt, so I closed my eyes and tried to imagine we were going to Ft. Worth. I did not want to accept the truth that he was in Chicago, anxiously waiting for me.

Nightly

You know, a nighty don't fit rightly on a child,
Might sound a bit wild; not wild at all to a pedophile.
Get something see-through, later I will enjoy.
Forced to choose which...
felt much like having to pick my own switch.
Thorns in every stitch.
A nighty?
I'm too small.
This doesn't feel good at all.
I made a public nuisance of myself.
He grabbed what he liked; and we left.
Mama stitched it to fit,
now that's some real sick
shit...

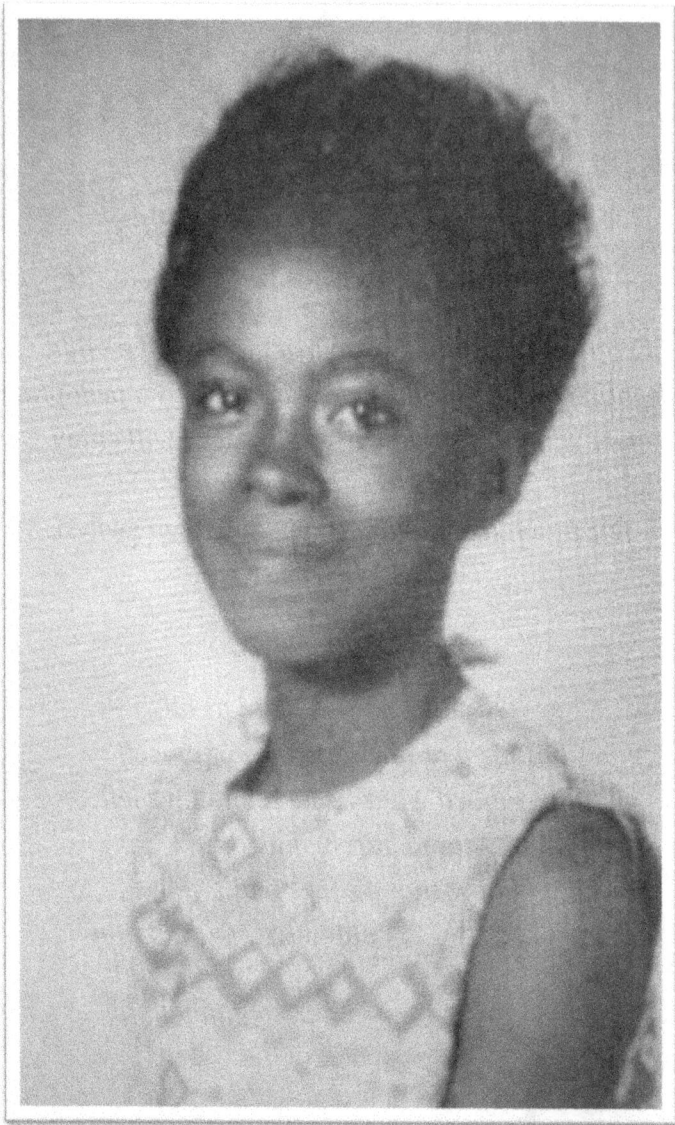

CHAPTER 7

FOURTEEN CANDLES

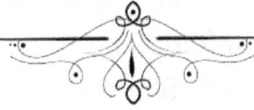

Mama was ill-prepared for the long trip in many ways. Firstly, our food supply had been depleted for hours. We rode for miles hungry and cold. The weather had changed, so the clothing we had wasn't sufficient. Without his interference, I had suddenly started to feel a closeness with my sisters. The need for warmth superseded my stubbornness toward bonding with them. My sister Tina was about five, and Dina was about three. We huddled together to stay warm.

Mama didn't think about the climate change. She had a baby on her hip, and according to birth records, she had one in the oven. Mama was traveling for the first time alone a thousand miles across the US, pregnant, with four children in tow. With not much more than the clothes on our backs. For the first time, she was free. She could have gone anywhere, but she obediently delivered us to him. She possibly realized that she should have left him waiting at the bus station and taken us somewhere safe instead. Something in her mind was very unsettling. Mama began wildly pacing up and down the aisle, rambling incoherently with my brother bobbing on her hip. I thought she was going to fall.

I finally convinced her to put him down. His pants were wet, and he was screaming his head off. I had never seen mama act that way. The bus driver asked her repeatedly to sit down. "What's wrong, ma'am?" he asked repeatedly. He, of course, got nowhere. At one point, he threatened to throw us off the bus if she didn't sit down and quiet the screaming baby. A lady was watching the situation unfold. Like an angel, she came from the back of the bus to our aid. She was able to calm mama down somehow until we made it to our final destination. The sound of the bus coming to a stop awakened me. All of us had fallen asleep, including mama.

The nice lady was holding my baby brother. As soon as my feet hit the ground after stepping off the bus, he was there, glaring at me. There was a pretty woman who had beautiful, naturally wavy black hair. She looked to be about twenty years old. "Hey, y'all, this my sista' Marie." I thought he was lying again. How could this beautiful woman be related to him? She hugged all of us and helped mama with our bags, while he barely acknowledged mama, or how she struggled traveling so far with no one to help with the "chullen." We were hungry, tired, and dirty. I had not given it a second thought about how we would be leaving the bus station. I assumed it would be by car.

He said, "We fixin' to get on a train. Y'all ain't never rode on a train befo." No, we hadn't. You can write a novel about the experiences we were deprived of growing up. The train hissed loudly and stopped in front of us. Taken aback by the newness of it all, we just stood frozen until he yelled at us, "Git on fo' we get left." We had to walk a short distance to the house. A very big woman greeted us at the door. He said, "That's yo' grandma Pat. That's my mama," with his big shit-eating grin all over his face.

Surprisingly his family was nothing like him. They helped mama get us cleaned up and put to bed. He had a family that loved him. It was beyond my comprehension, but they didn't know the person he really was. Once there, Mama miraculously calmed down and seemed fine again. Or was it her submissive character?

She seemed very content with how he ruled her. She welcomed him directing and wrecking our lives, regardless of how low he made her feel. Chicago was nothing at all like Bullard. Paved streets, traffic lights, trains, draw bridge lights, and activity in every direction. Brick houses were stacked on top of each other. A family was living below us. The whole way of living was different. Nobody had an outhouse or a well. Food came from the grocery store instead of having to stomach my meal being slaughtered right before my eyes. I wanted to be a city girl for sure.

I must have walked around with my eyes wide open for weeks. I had never seen buildings that disappeared into the skyline. I later learned they were called skyscrapers. I was unfamiliar with anything else a big city had to offer, for that matter. There were people selling food from carts on the street. Now that to me was what "going to town" meant. Tyler paled in comparison to this big city with flashing lights. It was like I had traveled to another time in just a few days.

Chicago's charm began to wear off. I felt betrayed once again by my own mama. All the times I needed her attention, she was detached and unavailable. Yet, her faculties were intact enough to transfer our school information from Texas to Illinois, hide our packed belongings, and secretly arrange transportation to the bus station, all without one mental break. J.N. Thorp Elementary was quite different from the country school I knew. An unfamiliar environment, but with the same fears, while pretending to be a normal kid.

Thinking back, I must have looked pretty pitiful and frail. Did anyone at school notice? Maybe they thought I was just shy and country. I was bullied for being intelligent, respectful, and my southern accent. Every time I responded to the teacher, "Yes sir," or "No sir," they died laughing.

Someone was always grabbing my graded work to announce, "Her smart ass got another A." The kids were loud, disruptive, and talked back to the teacher—another thing foreign to me. Where I came from, that type of disrespect was not tolerated. Had they known what my home life was like and how I fought my step monster every night, the bullying would have been quite unbearable.

Nothing they could say to me hurt more than what was waiting for me at home. They believed all Texans rode horses for transportation. If only they knew we were too poor to own a horse or had no running water until we arrived in Chicago. They teased me for any little thing. The only thing they knew about Texas was what they saw in the movies, which was fine with me. I started to imagine the life they taunted, imagining myself horseback, riding freely, away from it all, saddled with pain, but with determination, not to be broken. I was accustomed to meanness. Their comments rolled off me like water off a duck's back. "Arty is my name, and fucking motherfuckers up is my game." I had Dolomite in my head for those city kids. They didn't have a clue how tough I was or what I had lived through in the last six years.

Mama had taught me well how to ignore people. Double Dutch jump rope was one thing that could have taken me out for sure. My nerves had been shot for years. I had no interest in shaking myself up any further. Besides, I was not there at all for fun. Hell, I hadn't laughed very much in years. I think I had forgotten how to play. School was over for the summer about a month after we arrived, so I didn't have to deal with their silliness for long. There was a spare bedroom at his mama's house. It had previously been his younger brother's room. It reminded me of our black house in Bullard. The room was painted black with glow-in-the-dark stars all over the ceiling. Little did I know it would be a torture chamber for Mama and me.

I still remember the layout of the house. It was a shotgun house. The dining area was in the center, with a daybed pushed against the back wall near the kitchen. All five of us slept mushed together on that small daybed. If one person peed the bed, we all got wet. He needed a secluded area to do his dirty work. Unlike rooms at our house, these rooms had doors that locked. One night, he woke me by pulling on my arm. He led me to that dark room, leaving my siblings none the wiser, sleeping undisturbed.

Pulling me inside the room, he pushed me onto the bed next to mama. He then turned and locked the door with one swift move. Before I could focus my eyes, he was ripping my clothes

101

off. I thought mama was going to help him like she had done before, but mama started hitting and pushing him away from me. I had not witnessed her stand up to him.

I believe mama had made a deal with the devil on my behalf, and it had gotten out of hand. He was breaching their verbal contract and he was supposed to impregnate her only, not her daughter. In other words, he was not supposed to use his dick, violating me with his germ filled hands was the preauthorized limitation.

That's why she was helping me fight him. He had tried to do it in the barn (behind her back). His horny patience was growing thin. Raping his wife's daughter right in her face, and daring her to intervene was not beneath him. He had groomed her to not only accept it but to participate. He expected her to sit blindly and watch him ravish my tiny body. Mama had made a lot of bad choices while under the influence of mental illness, but on that night she came back to reality to save me.

His brother had left behind a stereo system with two tall speakers. He turned it on to drown out my screams and the commotion we were causing. Our cries empowered him. He pulled his thang out of his pants and started rubbing it, chasing me around the room.

I was more than terrified. I wanted to puke. Mama started hitting him in the back. It was a real-life horror show, but for him, it was comedy. It was a long night of us fighting him off. He groped, grabbed, and chased me around for hours; mama didn't give in as he expected. The only light in the room was coming through the window from the streetlights. It was very dark, like being outside at night in Bullard. A thick funk encapsulated that small room, making it hard to breathe. Time was running out for me; he wanted to teach me another "lesson."

I had been trying to find a way to tell his mama what had been happening since he married mama, but it had to be the right time. It's not something you can just blurt out to a stranger; she was his mother, after all. What if she didn't care?

What if she was just like mama and looked the other way or told me to stay in a kid's place? The beating that night was one of the worst ever. Probably because he had to fight both of us for the first time, whether it was a "fit" or a fit of anger, I was proud of her for once. I thought about getting a knife from the kitchen and killing him when he let us out. But I was too small to carry that out, and I knew it. So, my only hope was to tell his mama. After that, I just had to live until daylight, like I had done many times before. Mama had tried to deter him several times by encouraging him to get some rest for work, but he was relentless.

He finally rested for a couple of hours but instructed mama not to open the door and let me out. He was afraid his mama would see me leaving the room crying and beaten. Living under someone else's roof was getting to him. He couldn't freely do whatever he wanted. He had conditioned mama to allow his disgusting behavior, and now he was having to relinquish some of his powers. He could no longer beat his chest while roaring, "This my house, I do whatever I want, and ain't no motherfucker gonna stop me!" He was lashing out the only way he knew how. He relieved his stress by beating, molesting, and raping children. Finally, daybreak came as it always did.

I decided that had to be the day to open my mouth and tell Grandma Pat. He was inches away from raping me. It had been his goal for months, and he always got what he wanted eventually. Now that he had alienated us from mama's family, he intended to carry out his sick craving. I knew it. Mama knew it too. I had to stick to my plan. I had to get away from "my family." Smugly smiling, "See y'all this evenin'." He left for work, promising to finish what he started.

His mama could tell something was wrong with me when she saw me sitting with my head down. She asked mama what had happened. Mama told her I had got a whipping for cursing, that's all. His mama knew something wasn't right. When she was sleeping, she naively thought everyone else in the house was also sleeping. He wasn't. He had continued to touch me while looking over his shoulder in case she woke up to get something from the kitchen in the middle of the night. She would be horrified if she found her estranged son's hands in his stepdaughter's panties. "Come in my room for a minute, baby." She grabbed my hand and led me to her room. Mama didn't stop her. She sat on her bed and pulled me close to her. With the most pained expression I had seen on an adult, she softly asked, "Is that son of a bitch hurting you?"

I cried, "Yes, ma'am. He been hurting me for a long time!" She pulled my shirt up to see what she expected. He had whipped every inch of me with a belt. I was covered with welts. She immediately cried. She almost smothered me in her fat. She had a not-so-fresh smell, but it wasn't at all offensive.

She kept hugging me and crying. I could smell the snuff on her breath, but I could tell her compassion for me was real. I told her the short version of many years of torture. I said, "He tried to put his thang in me in a barn before we came here. That's why he brought us, so I can't tell." She wiped both of our tears with the same handkerchief, but I didn't mind. She held my face in her hands, looked into my eyes, and sobbed. She was overwhelmed with sympathy for me.

Crying with someone was a first. I had cried alone for years and never had someone console me. I loved her right away. She was taking my side against her own son. She told me to go clean myself up, and she was coming out to make breakfast. She said, "I promise you, God, is my witness. I'm not gonna let him hurt you in this house, ever again!" The words coming out of her mouth sounded like a foreign language. She was disciplining her grown son.

Grandma Pat was a strong black woman, not the kind to help mama fix a pot of grits, but she was not too afraid to stand up to him. Not only did she talk about what she would do, but she went above and beyond what most mamas would. Grandma Pat called the police and started the process of holding him accountable. For the first time, I felt my words meant something. She filled me with an unfamiliar confidence. Only now do I realize the impact his mother made on me. Chicago, Illinois, known as the Windy City, warmly welcomed me and gave me a whole new, bright outlook on life. Chicago offered me an unexpected promise.

Later that evening, a policeman knocked at the door. Grandma Pat's sister had arrived and let him in. Grandma Pat handed the policeman a sealed envelope and asked if he would like to have a seat. She whispered, "He will be walking through

105

the door any minute." I didn't catch on immediately. Mama was in the back tending to the kids.

As expected, he casually walked in. His cocky grin melted when he saw the officer. "What's going on?" he asked, all bug-eyed. Grandma Pat yelled, "You know what for! Stop playing stupid. You nasty dog!" The officer explained that he was not under arrest, but he needed to come to the police headquarters for questioning. "What fo?" he asked.

"Sir, collect your wife and the child in question and come with me." The officer loaded us three into the police car, and off we went to the Chicago police station.

As we three sat in the back seat, he whispered under his breath to mama, "You better not say shit." She nodded. I was thinking, "I'm not keeping quiet anymore." I thought I was finally going to be safe. I thought he was going to be locked away forever. From the police car, we were escorted into a room with a metal table and four chairs. Another officer followed us in and closed the door behind him. He motioned for us to sit. The officer was a white man, and his voice was very assertive. My thin body was covered in welts from the beating the night before. Giving us a slow once-over, I'm sure the hair on the back of his neck raised.

He observed before him a grungy, foul-smelling man, with his visibly pregnant, pitiful-looking wife, and a skinny shaking little girl, who looked like she had been to war. "Sir. Ma'am. Thanks for your cooperation. We received a frantic, disturbing call from your mother this morning. I know it was hard for her to have to call us again. Your brother has been in enough trouble." The officer had a pen and pad taking notes. He asked the basic

106

information about where we moved from and why? He lied, of course, mentioning something about needing to find work. The officers didn't let him finish with his lies. He interrupted, "Your mother provided a handwritten statement, and I believe every word. Ma'am, did your husband beat this child?" The officer asked. Softy mama responded, "Yes sir, she was cursing and talking back."

Ma'am, has this man sexually assaulted and attempted to rape her?" He looked directly at me while quizzing mama. I was nodding yes. "No sir, he didn't," mama lied. Finally, the officer calmly stated, "I had to allow you to come clean and show some dignity, but I see that's beneath you. I don't believe a damn word coming out of your lying mouths. I'm looking at this kid, and I know the truth. How old is she, ma'am?" Mama held her head down and replied, "She is eleven." The officer sighed loudly and reluctantly. He told us the law was that I had to be at least twelve years old before he could accept my statement without my parents' verification of its validity. I was pissed.

He leaned forward, "This child confided to your mother that for many years you have fondled her and that you almost raped her in a barn. You sorry piece of shit, I want you out of my city. Your mama has expressed in this statement you are no longer welcome in her home as well." The officer got down on one knee, took my hands in his, and said the sweetest words I had ever heard. "You are a brave little girl. You keep talking until you turn twelve. I'm sorry my hands are tied today. If you're still around, come see me." The officer turned and snarled, "Child molesters make my flesh crawl, get him out of my sight."

He was as quiet as a church mouse in the back of the police car on the ride back home. The officer had made him feel a tiny bit of the shame he had made me feel a million times. He didn't like being degraded; imagine that. He was a bit taken aback. No one had the balls to cross him before, especially a woman. When we got back to Grandma Pat's, he was furious. His manly prowess had returned. "I got my own shit in Bullard," he proudly proclaimed. They immediately started packing to go back to where it all started. I couldn't imagine going back to the black house of horror, back to dark silence.

Grandma Pat sobbed pitifully while giving him a piece of her mind, "You tricked me into helping you. I want you gone as soon as you get paid. Lee is sleeping with me until y'all leave. You had better not lay one hand on her!" He yelled, "Fuck you, you fat bitch! We leavin' next week after I get my last paycheck!" She said, "Naw negro, you leaving sooner than that! I will pay for y'all's tickets back to Texas. I will have the company mail your check. I can't stand to look at you another day. A week is too long!"

In less than a week, we were back at the train stop. On our way back to the Greyhound bus station, I was more than ready to go back to Texas. But Grandma Pat kept her eyes on me while still in her house. I slept with her those few nights until we left. She had to have weighed at least three hundred pounds. She put me between herself and the wall. Her massive body was a barrier, shielding me from whoever might try to come for me during the night. I got the best sleep in those few days than I had gotten in years. Every night before bed, she talked to me like I was grown, but in a respectful way.

She confided that she had not raised him. His father had raised him, "He is just like his daddy. I want you to go back home and tell your people to help you." She was a godsend.

We all know the phrase, "God puts some people in your life for a reason." No one would have called the police if I had never gone to Chicago. But sadly, I didn't know it was an option. I wouldn't have known words like fondling, child molester, and dignity.

That move was meant to isolate me but had provided valuable information I needed to know instead. Once again, what he intended as evil had turned in my favor. There is a whole world of people out there who don't support child abuse. Some people mothers will speak truth to power, even if the powerful figure is their son. And not just throw words against the wall but make a solid effort to stop the madness. And most of all, I learned there are laws in place to help children.

Grandma Pat made me understand he had learned his mean and sexually inappropriate behaviors from his father, giving me a clearer understanding of his persona. At the same time, she encouraged me to seek help. She put the burden on me to find a way out; the officer had done the same. His sister avoided coming around before we departed. She wanted nothing to do with him either.

The bus ride home was quite different. Mama was back to her usual calm, but he was quite chill himself. He would say something nasty about his mama to mama every so often. He glared at me, and I glared back. I knew he couldn't beat me on the bus. Once back there, I knew I had to free myself somehow. Mama had to choose a side, and it sure wasn't mine.

Anybody that didn't know what I had been going through soon would. I planned to make sure of it when we returned to Texas. I should clarify that I planned to press the issue. Mama became more withdrawn. Her reality was too much for any woman, let alone one weakened by mental illness and domestic abuse. She mostly sat and stared into space. I'm sure postpartum depression plagued her in rapid succession. We had barely made it back to Bullard before she was back at the hospital giving birth to her fifth child.

We were literally at his disposal. He made sure we all felt like trash. I had started planning to leave by any means necessary. I began smuggling a few clothes to Daddy's house. He told me where to put them, but he was too much of a coward to do anything more than that. Cousin Hartie lived about a ten-minute walk from us. I begged mama to let me ask to use her phone to call her sister, to tell her we were back in Bullard safely, because I was sure they had been worried about us.

When I got Sister on the line, I blurted out, "Please come get me. Call Mack, please! Please! I told her about his mama calling the police when we were in Chicago. "The policeman said I can press charges when I turn twelve." I was breathless from running the whole way. I don't remember how many calls I made pleading for help. Cousin Hartie was happy to open her screen door for me every time. I had stopped getting permission from mama. So, I ran down the road every chance I got to make my call. Sometimes it just rang, but I kept calling. When I think about it now, having a party-line probably helped put the heat on the family to get off their asses and come save me.

He had toned down his indecency considerably, he wasn't coming in my room at night, but he was still groping me during the day to prove he was again in charge. Shortly after we returned, I started seventh grade. I was not at all interested in school. The new books and not even the dictionary got my attention. I wanted to leave Bullard. That was all I cared about. One morning shortly after he left for work, mama told me I wasn't going to school that day. I didn't ask why. I was exhausted and had lost interest in everything, including school.

I went to sit on the porch and enjoyed not having to dodge him for a change. Then, a shiny new green car pulled up beside the house. Pete and Mack got out. When I saw her face. I ran to her, almost knocking her off her feet. My calls for help were not ignored. Mack said, "Sis, you gonna let her go? I will take good care of her. You know it's best." Mama nodded, "Okay Mack, take her. I'm tired." Apparently, mama had made some calls herself when he wasn't around. I think Cousin Hartie had intervened as well.

I was finally being rescued. Tears poured down my face. Bittersweet tears nonetheless, leaving them behind saddened me because I knew he would take his anger out on all of them. Watching the house disappear as Pete drove away felt so good. It was like the best dream, except I was wide awake. I was headed to my new life in Ft. Worth with Mack. Pete drove us all the way to Ft. Worth. They were not taking any chances of him tracking us down in that piece of shit truck of his. My neck hurt from turning around to see if he had caught up to us somehow.

Mack lived alone in a small one-bedroom house. She bought a twin bed for me. It was like having a personal bodyguard. I could sleep undisturbed. The best part of all was the old-style claw foot bathtub; it was big and deep. Mack made me a bubble bath almost every night.

With no kids of her own, she poured all her love into me. As I mentioned before, her clothes were always beautiful, and she liked to smell good, so she shopped for me too. She brought color to my world in every way. We shopped for school clothes. She put them on layaway because she didn't make much money. Aunt Mack believed in looking and feeling her best, and she instilled those qualities in me.

She enrolled me in Meadowbrook Middle School. A new school, new clothes, and new friends were just what the doctor ordered. In seventh grade, I finally felt loved and protected as I should have been all along. For the first time, I was examined by a doctor. Mack provided the doctor with a handwritten letter mama had given her giving her guardianship.

Mack wanted to make sure I was okay in every way she knew how. No more horrible home remedies that I'd grown accustomed to in Bullard, like cow chip tea. For you unknowing city dwellers, that's dried cow manure (shit) wrapped in a cloth, boiled on the stove with some wild leaves, and it supposedly cures the common cold and fever. Home remedies have benefits, like sitting over a steaming bucket to relieve constipation. However, my digestive issues may have resulted from consuming powdered eggs, powdered milk, canned beef, and that block of cheese provided by the government for the impoverished. God only knows what that jelly-like substance was in the cans of meat.

He wanted me to gain weight, "Damn, gal. You gone blow away." So, he made mama give me something from the Watkin man (door-to-door medical and personal supplies) to make me gain weight. It was thick and white, and it tasted awful. Fattening me up wasn't going to make me a woman. I didn't gain a pound. If anything, I got skinnier from the stress, which led to a poor appetite. Mama made the best homemade chicken and dumplings from scratch That was my favorite meal. But for the most part, I did not enjoy eating at all because my stomach was always queasy, or I had a huge lump in my throat from holding back tears.

It has taken many years of maturity to understand the agony mama had to live with after that critical decision and all the guilt she must have felt for allowing it to go on for so many years. I have repeatedly, harshly misjudged her motherly instincts, without having the benefit of truly knowing her. Now as a mature woman, I can grasp what as a child, I misinterpreted as her being dismissive and cold toward me.

Mama's eyes had said it all as I hugged her goodbye. She was expressionless, but I saw defeat in her eyes. He had emotionally beaten her down to the dirt, literally, and had forced her hand in sending her firstborn child away. That had to have hurt her tremendously. She forfeited her parental rights to save me, while keeping her other children in harm's way.

Months passed, and I began to settle into my new home. Then, I had my first fight with someone my age. A girl decided to test my survival skills. When we got off the bus she pushed me for no reason. I think she just wanted to show off by teasing the new girl. Well, long story short, I took thirteen years of pent-up frustration out on her face. The fight started and ended before I knew what had happened. Some of the kids followed me home. They were calling me The Karate Kid. I had my first fair fight. "All my life I've had to fight Harpo."

I ran inside crying, but I had quickly whooped her ass. The next day, I had an entourage of kids from the neighborhood waiting to walk with me to the bus stop. I didn't want to fight again, but I wasn't backing down either. The girl was sporting a big black eye. She said, "I just want to let you know you gave me a black eye." I don't know why she felt the need to state the obvious, but I didn't have any more problems with her after that.

This investigation of myself has revealed some more startling information. I was already twelve years old when we went to the police station. I wrote down how old I was at the start of each school year. Sure enough, I was already twelve. It seems mama had lost track of time. It's quite possible, considering all that had transpired in her life. I don't believe she lied intentionally. He surely didn't know, nor care when my birthday was, and he definitely wasn't capable of calculating how many years and months from December 1960 to June 1973.

Not celebrating birthdays was probably a blessing in disguise. He would have found a way to make it an excruciating memory for sure. But that misinformation, at least, wasn't wasted. It would get us back to Texas. I didn't want to get trapped in Chicago with his family even though his mama was the first to stand up against him. I would not have gotten the same recognition had we stayed bumps on a log in Bullard. Judging

114

from his prison rap sheet, it was only a matter of time before he raped me. The move to Chicago backfired. He didn't get the outcome he hoped for, nor the support.

All the pretty clothes in the world can't remove the effects of childhood trauma. Like most Black families, Mack overlooked my need for therapy. Seeking professional help for depression is almost unheard of and costly. Most Black families cannot afford the treatment. So, as many do, we put on a fake smile, we cover up our emotions in the finest fabrics, and we adorn ourselves with silver and gold to deflect the pain we feel inside. We pretend everything is everything.

December 14, 1974, it was on a Saturday —my first birthday party. I'll never forget it. Cake, ice cream, hot dogs, chips, kids, gifts, all in honor of me. Mack loved special occasions. Her extravagant nature was evident in whatever she presented. She wrapped a lot of boxes and placed random objects in them to make it look like I had more gifts than she could afford. She did that at Christmas as well. And she loved a speech. "I love you, Lee. Make a wish."

I burst out crying, which freaked the kids out. I'm sure they were thinking I was too old to be sobbing at my birthday party like a toddler. I was overwhelmed with emotion. When they sang Happy Birthday, I cried even more. They were happy tears of joy, freedom, and most all, for once, I felt like a kid. I saw how the other teenagers were so carefree and happy-go-lucky. I, on the other hand, was never mindless or unconcerned. Feelings of impending doom followed me around for months. I was unaccustomed to happiness. I continuously waited for "the next shoe to fall."

Blowing out the candles, I wished for more days like that day and the ability to be a carefree kid again with nothing to worry about. I wished I knew my real daddy and that he wanted to know me as well. Later that night, I asked Aunt Mack if she knew where he might be. She assured me she would try to locate his "sorry ass." The best gift of all was meeting Deb. She was Mack's best friend's sister. We were the same age. Her birthday was two weeks after mine. So, I had someone my age to laugh and be silly with. I could tell her anything. She was like a big sister because she knew about city life, and she had the freedom to explore the city without an adult. I, on the other hand, was a country bumpkin.

Deb had the bubbliest personality, and was a master in the art of high siding (shit talking). I was her willing understudy, and high siding became my forte as well. Being around her made me happy. We both had potty mouths and cursed just for the fun of it when we were out of the earshot of adults. Every day after that felt like my birthday. Mack was always buying me something to make me feel pretty. My life was finally showing signs of normalcy. I was able to rest, although recurring nightmares continued for years.

Fourteen years old and ready to take on the world, I slowly began to feel valued with Mack's love and encouragement. I felt clean again, and most of all, I was safe. Mack was a real mama bear, constantly asking if I was okay, almost to the point of being annoying. We talked about everything under the sun, but never about what happened to me. Mack was a very emotional person. We spared each other feelings by not bringing up the past.

School was out for the summer, Mack was at work, when I heard a car pull up and stop, and the sound of someone closing a car door. I heard voices, and then the car drove away. There was a knock at the door. Mack had instructed me never to answer the door while she was at work. Rarely did anyone come to visit unannounced, so immediately, I was on guard. I heard mama's voice yelling my name. "Lee, you in there?" I was terrified. She had come without warning for a reason, and that was to take me back to him. I ran and hid in the closet.

After knocking violently for several minutes, the knocking stopped. I stayed hidden in the closet. Checking the time, I knew Mack would be getting off the city bus soon. I ran to meet her at the corner as I often did. Mama was sitting at the end of the street near the corner store, to my surprise. She was watching and waiting for us to come home. Like clockwork, Mack was approaching from the bus. I ran toward her, and mama followed. Mack asked her, "Why are you here?" Mama said, "I need to take Lee back home now." Mack yelled, "Hell naw! She is doing good here. He put you up to this?"

Mama grabbed one arm, and Mack grabbed the other one. They began jerking me from side to side, playing tug of war with my body. Mack was a force to reckon with, and she was a scrapper. She yanked me so hard I thought she had pulled my arm out of the socket. Someone seeing the commotion called the police because a cop car drove up. "What's going on here?" The officer asked while assessing the situation. I was shaking like a leaf on a tree. Mama and Mack were out of breath. Both were gasping for air. Mama started explaining to the officer that my stay with her sister was never meant to be permanent, and it was time for me to return home and that I was refusing to come with her.

I instantly flashed back to things not ending well for me with the police in Chicago, so immediately, I was afraid. I was prepared for the policeman to return me, a minor, to mama's custody, regardless of the note Mack carried in her purse. Finally, staying in a child's place was over, I screamed, "Mama, tell him why I came here in the first place!"

The officer didn't give her a chance to respond. Instead, he stated, "I have never seen a child more terrified of her own mother. I don't know or care why she is here. I can see the terror in her eyes, so she's staying put. I don't see a vehicle. How did you get here?"

Mama said she had come by bus and got a taxi from the bus station. The policeman informed her if she returned, she would be charged with trespassing and child endangerment. He put mama in the police car and dropped her off where she asked. I believe he was nearby and had her arrive by taxi to throw us off. All I know is she was gone, and I was relieved. Mack and I went home. She threw away the torn dress and gave me a bubble bath.

I didn't write or speak to mama for many years after that near recapture. Mack moved us to the other side of town shortly after that scare. There was no way she was letting him find me again. I believe mama was relieved the officer prevented her from aiding her pedophile husband again. I'm sure he gave her ten kinds of hell for showing up without me in tow. That disturbing part of my life was physically over in 1974, but sadly, it cannot be erased from my memory. When life gives you a pedophile, you devise an escape plan.

HARDSHIP

Innocence and beauty subjected...

Minds forever altered and affected,
Pathways mindlessly misguided.
Families indefinitely divided,
Sly as a fox...
Hanging around the toy box.
Such pleasure you take in our pain.
There's no chance you will refrain.
Planning to destroy our lives.
Regardless of your evil guise
Like the phoenix, we rise!

CHAPTER 8

PRIMARY TARGET

I believe I am the first of many children that were victimized by this man. Unwillingly I assisted in providing a curriculum for his master classes in pedophilia. I was his protégé, providing a blueprint of tried and true plans for future chosen victims. Therefore, I feel some sense of motherhood, I want to hug each and every one of you. Purposefully recalling the trauma and relentless abuse I endured, for obvious reasons I prefer not. I have desperately tried to remove those memories from my memory bank. Past traumatic experiences have a way of rearing their unwelcome ugly heads when least expected. There are always news headlines sparking memories such as sex trafficking, Amber alerts, kidnapping, and the abuse of innocent children.

Pedophile, MAD (minor attracted person), child molester, child predator—no matter the address, they all are disgusting, repulsive beings, crippling children's futures and forever altering their life experiences. The justice system allows them to offend repeatedly. Prison terms should carry life sentences. This trauma's effects are a lifelong struggle. Therefore, life without parole for pedophiles is not far-fetched in my mind. Childhood trauma predisposes one to chronic illnesses in adulthood.

I had gallstones removed at age nineteen, irritable bowel syndrome diagnosed in my early twenties, cataracts in both eyes in my late fifties, followed by arthritis, high blood pressure, and of course, years of depression and anxiety. Chronic illness is often overlooked as a predetermined side effect of childhoods trauma; more commonly expected is the difficulty of forming interpersonal relationships, promiscuity, drug abuse, and even suicide. Psychiatric therapy for me, though brief, only made me feel worse. An hour of rehashing painful memories, followed by days of the same, at home alone, until the next session was not therapeutic for me. I had to train my brain not to let paralyzing thoughts ruin my day.

Reliving those days to complete this mission has not been easy at all. I have spent countless days stuck on a reminiscence I have had to step away and reevaluate whether I should share my history. By far, writing this memoir has been the most therapeutic for me and has made me realize it is never too late for professional therapy. Unexpectedly I have a clearer understanding of how it all came to pass so easily and why it lasted as long as it did. Mama was ill and lacked the support she needed to pull through.

I hope to encourage self-love and empowerment to victims of childhood trauma. Feelings of self-worth can be hard to acquire without a steadfast support system. As the saying goes, "Everything happens for a reason." The only positive I can see is me being an example for someone else, who may feel it's too late to speak their truth. Truth is power; it can release your inner demons for the world to see. God will thereby place people in your life who will positively embrace you. It's incredible how one person can significantly impact your life, negatively or positively.

The American Psychological Association states that an adult who engages in sexual activity with a child performs a criminal and immoral act that can never be considered normal or socially acceptable behavior. In addition, according to the Adverse Childhood Experiences Study (ACE), the rougher your youth, the higher the score is likely to be and the risk for later health problems.

There is a list of tasks that explore adverse childhood experiences, linking them to various adult conditions. I encourage referring to CDC's ACE Study website. Surround yourselves with people who understand and believe in you. Someone you can confide in, or psychiatric therapy can significantly mitigate the long-term effects.

For many years, I studied and read anything I could to help me understand the mind of a pedophile. I needed to know why it happened to me. Why any child? Not once have I found any logical, reasonable explanation because sex with a child is unnatural. Unfortunately, nationwide there is a bottomless pit of child predators; a new one is born every day. If only there were some way to detect who they are at birth, maybe we could handle the situation.

I watched a documentary in Iraq where young girls are sold into temporary marriages called pleasure marriages so grown men can legally abuse them. Just as quickly as they are married, they are discarded like trash. Many end up in prostitution or commit suicide. Girls as young as ten years old are selected. The exploitation of children is a booming business worldwide with no end in sight. Men and women travel overseas to feel safe to abuse children. Where they believe the chance of long jail terms is less likely. The lengths a pedophile will go, and the miles he/she will travel purposefully to scar a child for life is truly mind-blowing.

Information I found online shows that in 2006, President Bush signed a new law requiring convicted child molesters to be listed on a national internet database and face felonies for not updating their whereabouts. Child advocates have called this bill the most sweeping sex offender legislation to target pedophiles in many years, the first national online listing available to the public and searchable by zip code. In addition, much harsher punishments are now handed down for sexually assaulting children, including the possibility of the death penalty for murdering a child.

By creating the national child abuse registry, investigators can do background checks on adoptive and foster parents before they are approved to receive a child into their custody. The law would establish a federal DNA database of material collected from convicted molesters, federal funding for states to track pedophiles, and allow victims to sue their molesters. The law imposes a mandatory thirty-year sentence for raping a child. In addition, a mandatory ten-year penalty for sex trafficking involving children and luring them into prostitution increases minimum sentences for molesters who travel between states.

With these laws and many others meant to protect children, they unfortunately, will always suffer emotional, physical, and or sexual abuse at the hands of adults intended to protect them. The school curriculum should include routine one on one discussions about abuse. Sometimes, a kid is waiting for someone to ask the hard questions. "Is there anything at all that makes you very sad or scared?"

Parents must do their part as well to teach their children personal boundaries. The child may often not recognize the offense as something bad right away. Mainly if the abuse has been occurring all their lives, they may think it's normal. Sadly, as long as children are born into this world, many will be harmed in unimaginable ways. In this so-called "cancel culture," can we find a way to cancel pedophilia? Pedophiles cancel childhoods every day. With every new day comes new opportunities to learn new information and a chance to meet that one person who can change your whole life in the most positive way imaginable.

CHAPTER 9

Epilogue

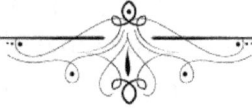

I have referred to Mama, Mack, Bobby, and Daddy in the past tense throughout this memoir because they are all deceased. May of 1993, Daddy died first. He was seventy-seven years old. According to birth and death records, Daddy's daddy lived in Tyler and died there in 1976. He, like Bobby, was eighteen when 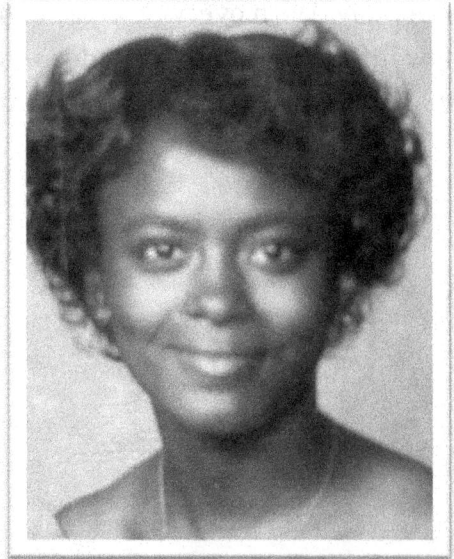 Daddy was born and had walked away as well. Generation upon generation of poor examples of father figures. I recommend *Ancestry.com* as a great way to find accurate, literally buried genetic information.

December 17, that same year, Mack fought and lost a short battle with colon cancer. She passed away in my home. Pete was the only one of her siblings present. Ironically, the three of us were together again, but this time, it was me helping Mack find comfort, by helping her get to her final resting place. I wanted my children to know the importance of family and the family response in a crisis. So we banned together, and together, and we respectfully laid her to rest at the Corinth Baptist Church cemetery, next to Daddy and Madea as she requested.

Her picture is the only one I display on my kitchen counter. I see her and feel her presence every day. I dreamed big because she made me understand the importance of achieving in school. Simply put, she made me the compassionate, reliable, independent, clean freak I am today. She's wearing a purple dress in the photo because purple was her favorite color. I chose that picture because her hair had grown back after chemotherapy. That photo is a symbol of her "never give up" spirit. Mack always presented herself in the best light possible to the world. She treated her illness no differently. Something as simple as doing the laundry reminds me of her. She would say, "Always take care of your things, and they will last."

Mama was sixty-two when she passed away nine years later, June 18, 2002, of a fatal heart attack. Her heart had been attacked a million times. The invisible puncture wounds were deep. "If a tree falls in a forest and no one is around to hear it, does it make a sound?" Only now do I fully comprehend the depths of hell she silently endured. That peacefulness was a pressure cooker. She held in a lifetime of toxic emotions. She chewed and swallowed her pain and the pain of her children her entire life. My biggest regret is not knowing she needed me as much as I needed her.

July 20, 2011, Bobby passed away nine years after mama. He died from lung cancer. He was "full of hot air" for sure. He preached one thing and lived another. I finally met him when I was seventeen. Mack arranged it, of course. Finding kind words for my daddy, a "man of the cloth" is difficult, so I will thank him for my genetic makeup and move on without exposing all the distasteful things he did to me after being persuaded to come forward as "my real daddy."

I want to focus on the positives from his passing. Instantly I bonded with his brother and wife. We have formed an everlasting connection. I call him Uncle, and I call her aunt, mama, sister, Connie. She is all those things to me and more. They are like the parents I never had.

For the past ten years, they have been prayer warriors, my support system, and they make me feel more special than they will ever know. Uncle is a motivational, inspirational, clean eating powerhouse. God placed Uncle and Aunt Connie in my life, no doubt about it. They wholeheartedly encourage and support this journey of healing by welcoming total transparency.

Uncle admitted he had always known of my existence and how Bobby willingly shirked he responsibilities. He and Aunt Connie noticed me sitting with the family. He said he was determined to find out who I was. He wondered if I could be Bobby's illegitimate daughter. His intuition was spot on. Several months later, they invited me to visit their home in California. Actually, I kind of invited myself. Something about them was special to me as well. That spur-of-the-moment visit was the beginning of something special.

Uncle asked me questions about my childhood growing up, which led to an unexpected, very powerful acceptance of Jesus as my Lord and Savior in his home on March 13th, 2012. I opened up to them about my horrible childhood. Uncle explained to me the meaning of forgiveness. I had only been told, "You need to forgive him." I did not understand forgiveness before that. My forgiving has nothing to do with his salvation at all. Uncle even prayed for the man I have hated most of my life.

He and Aunt Connie were the first to have an honest conversation about what happened to me. Uncle drove me to his favorite Christian bookstore. He bought a large print side-by-side of the King James Version amplified bible for me. Instantaneously, they not only accept me as family, but they also genuinely care for my inner well-being. He had it engraved with my full name in gold letters. Uncle and Aunt Connie hold a most special place in my heart.

After leaving Bullard, my life continued on a fast track. In 1977, I had my first child at sixteen. I'm sure no one expected that with such a strict morally sound upbringing. One year later, I graduated from high school at seventeen. I was determined to finish high school to provide a life for myself. My main focus was to be independent. Teenage pregnancy cannot be taken lightly, so don't use me as an example on that. I longed for someone to love and to feel love in return. I needed connectedness and a purpose in my life, so selfishly, I became a teenage mom. This is the perfect opportunity to publicly raise my hand to a woman's choice to have or not have children.

Knowing firsthand what being deprived of basic needs can do to hinder a child's growth, both emotionally and physically, I have done my due diligence to make sure first of all my children's needs were met, and no one hurt them that lives to tell about it. Children need to understand that it takes a village. Some things that happen at home may need to be shared with another trusted family member or a person of authority. There are checks and balances to every situation; parenting is no different. There would be no need for CPS if the village remains intact.

August 1979, I graduated from All Saints School of Vocational Nursing. I was one of the youngest in the class. One of the instructors had no qualms about informing me and two other Black females that we were there only because the school was obligated by law to have a certain number of blacks. So we understood clearly that we were not welcome. Nevertheless, we all graduated and got our licenses to prove we not only deserved to be there but were smart enough to stay. I have had a gratifying nursing experience over the last forty-two years. I have served the medical community for more than four decades very well.

My first year of nursing, I worked tirelessly with ENT cancer patients. After about two years of that, I had had all I could stand. For many years I worked extensively with MHMR services, both at the Ft. Worth State school and transition to community living. I think I have been subconsciously filling the need to give back to some of the most vulnerable humans.

For about five years, I was an outpatient hospice nurse. I thought for sure it was my calling until I heard someone else say it. I found an entry in my journal from those days. I wrote, "Being a part of the love I witnessed today makes me bitter. I want a close family, too." When it works like it is supposed to, family structure is awe-inspiring to someone who's never had it. Over and over again, I witnessed family closeness. But honestly, I was a bit jealous.

For about five years, I worked in plasmapheresis. I learned countless ways lives are saved with plasma and its components. As a physician's substitute, the position I held required me to travel to North Carolina for a one-month training. Although the job came with a lot of responsibility and long hours, it was another enriching nursing experience.

For the first time, the center ran a successful rabies program under my supervision. It made me proud, being told I exuded the professionalism and confidence necessary to head the program. I traveled to Phoenix, Arizona, for training and was indeed able to spearhead that center's first rabies program successfully. Fifteen years later, I still like reading the reference letters from the Dr.'s I trained under. Six years and a million overtime hours later, they fired me for working my ass off.

I have been a pediatric home health nurse for the past fifteen years. My life has come full circle. The gratitude I feel for being able to bring comfort to God's most fragile children is immeasurable. The love I receive in return is priceless. Ironically, I am with my patient in his elementary classroom. I have a chance to experience elementary school all over again. At sixty-one years old, I am living my best life in elementary school. Look at God. Won't He do it!

I constantly dreamed of going far away while he planned to anchor me in Bullard. He intended to hobble me mentally so that if I did escape, I would be useless. My dreams have taken me from Bullard to Ft. Worth and far beyond. I have had rum punch in

Roatan, Honduras, and swam with the dolphins. I have had Mai Tai's in Hawaii and tea in a castle in the Czech Republic. I have been to The Port of Spain and danced in the streets of Trinidad and Tobago. I had the pleasure of visiting New York before 9/11 and experienced getting dizzy in The Sears Towers. There is not one thing that was taken from me that I have not reclaimed, gained back, or experienced.

Any flaw in my character might be necessary for my sustainability; therefore, I am my own best friend. For an old broad, I'm still fine. I can pass for forty-something on a good day. I don't look like the hell I've been through. For that, I am grateful. I'm playful and content. God has sustained my life in every way. Of course, I have had struggles, as is expected. I have made terrible choices, and as sure as I sit here will no doubt make more. I have learned mainly by trial and error. Had it not been for God, the errors would have taken me out.

As a consenting adult, I didn't know a damn thing about real life, real feelings, or real emotions. I grew up observing "pretend" relationships built on deception. I had no idea what real love looked or felt like. I've had one-night stands and two-day relationships, married, divorced, and remarried. I have made many mistakes, but I've been conditioned to use every stumbling block as a steppingstone. Nothing for me has been easy; therefore, I finally give myself grace. I am far from perfect, but I accept my shortcomings as room to grow. I know for sure I deserve every good thing life has to offer, and I am receiving it every day.

I have closed my cold case #12141960

Finding: Absence of Strong Family Leadership leading to the Breakdown of The Village.

1. "It takes a village to raise a child" is an African proverb that means that an entire community of people must provide for and interact positively with children for those children to experience and grow in a safe and healthy environment. (Wikipedia)

2. My village at birth was rather large but not sustainable. The fathers did not uphold their responsibilities and did not lay a sturdy foundation, causing the entire village to eventually disassemble. A village has to have a leader. In those days, men were considered the head of the household and expected to provide for and protect the family. Unfortunately, my father and grandfather left the gate open for "the boogeyman" to ravage and divide the village.

Many women in the South were expected to marry, have babies, and be taken care of by their husbands. When they were left to think for themselves, many stuck to the belief a man completed them, thereby making them settle for whoever pretended to love them. Behind every strong man is a good woman. What kind of woman is behind the weak man? An even weaker woman, perhaps?

Through *Ancestry.com* and Uncle's honesty, I have come to realize I come from a long line of fatherless fathers. It turns out their father also went to great lengths to avoid his parental responsibilities. None of the men that impacted my life were guided by their fathers to be upstanding men.

Daddy was my first protector, he failed miserably, but he never pretended to love anybody. He was a very unhappy man, and it showed. He coined the phrase, "I shoulda pissed you out to the ants." He often yelled that to one of his beloved children. Those two things cannot happen simultaneously. What a term of endearment to bark at your kids. Something about that tells me Daddy realized he had fathered too many children, and if he had it his way, he might have discarded a few of them.

To the fathers who might believe their presence is necessary: this is a page from www.Pediatricassociates.com.

Fathers and Emotional Development

Fathers, like mothers, are pillars in the development of a child's emotional well-being. Children look to their fathers to lay down the rules and enforce them. They also look to their fathers to provide a feeling of security, both physical and emotional. Children want to make their fathers proud, and an involved father promotes inner growth and strength. Studies have shown that when fathers are affectionate and supportive, it greatly affects a child's cognitive and social development. It also instills an overall sense of well-being and self-confidence.

Fathers Set the Bar for Relationships with Others

Fathers not only influence who we are inside, but how we have relationships with people as we grow. The way a father treats his child will influence what he or she looks for in other people. Friends, lovers, and spouses will all be chosen based on how the child perceived the meaning of the relationship with his or her father. The patterns a father sets in the relationships with his children will dictate how his children relate with other people.

Fathers and Their Daughters

Young girls depend on their fathers for security and emotional support. A father shows his daughter what a good relationship with a man is like. If a father is loving and gentle, his daughter will look for those qualities in men when she's old enough to begin dating. If a father is strong and valiant, she will relate closely to men of the same character.

Fathers and Their Sons

Unlike girls, who model their relationships with others based on their father's character, boys model themselves after their father's character. Boys will seek approval from their fathers from a very young age. As human beings, we grow up by imitating the behavior of those around us; that's how we learn to function in the world. If a father is caring and treats people with respect, the young boy will grow up much the same. When a father is absent, young boys look to other male figures to set the "rules" for how to behave and survive in the world.

Theimportantcite.com explains the importance of family/ the village.

1. Families set the stage for future relationships

The very first relationship a child has is with their parents and any siblings. Whether healthy or not, these relationships provide a model for what future relationships will look like. It's often not a conscious decision, but for better or worse, people often choose partners and friends based on how similar they are to their family. Family dynamics repeat themselves and reinforce beliefs about relationships and self.

2. During challenging times, people need a family they can rely on

When life gets hard, people need support. This can be emotional and/or financial support. Someone going through rough times will turn to their family if they trust them to provide encouragement and love. Feeling accepted and understood during a personal crisis is a basic need for people. Families – whether traditional or chosen – can provide that.

3. Families can be an essential source of affection and encouragement

In good or bad times, families can provide the affection and encouragement a person needs to be content. It can be difficult to find friends or purpose in adulthood. If a person has a strong family, they'll always be able to find the love and support they need. With their family behind them, a person will find the motivation and courage for success. On the other side, if a person isn't getting love and support from a family structure, they'll feel lonely, depressed, and even hopeless.

4. Families foster a sense of belonging to something greater than oneself

Families are hubs of tradition. Many families carry on traditions through the years by sharing stories from the past. This creates connections with family members that aren't around anymore. A person who grows up in this type of family feels like they belong to something bigger than themselves. They'll pride in being a member of a community that's gone through hardships and triumphs.

5. People raised in close families develop healthier relationships throughout their lives

Research supports that people from close-knit families go on to enjoy close relationships later in life. Psychological Science published a long-running study in 2016 that looked at men's relationships. Researchers learned that men who grew up in nurturing families developed stronger relationships than men who didn't have accepting families. They managed their emotions well and maintained a closer connection with their partners.

6. Family relationships are linked to a person's mental health

There have been many studies on the importance of family time, specifically dinner time. While families can still be healthy even if they don't eat dinner together every night, there is a correlation between this time together and a young person's wellbeing. In Pediatrics, one study discovered that kids who ate with their families regularly were less likely to show depression symptoms. On the other side of the spectrum, research shows that negative family relationships can trigger or worsen mental health issues.

7. Quality time with family is linked to better academic performance

The National Center on Addiction and Substance Abuse at Columbia University conducted a series of studies on family dinner time. One study showed that kids who eat dinner with their family less than three times were twice as likely to get Cs or below in school. On the other hand, kids who had family dinners 5-7 times a week did much better. Of course, there are other factors at play, but families that value dinners together likely value other positive family interactions.

8. Families teach important life lessons

Families are the first place where children learn how to manage their emotions, interact with others, and communicate. It's also the first setting where kids learn about consequences, either positive or negative. Parents are responsible for guiding their children, providing life lessons that will be remembered for years to come. These lessons form a big part of a person's worldview and how they believe the world works.

9. Families teach values

Along with life lessons, people learn a value system within their family structure. They learn what their family defines as right or wrong, as well as what's important to the community. These values become ingrained and form a foundational part of a person's identity. Values affect how a person treats others, how they view themselves, and what they see as their purpose in life.

10. Healthy families form the backbone of a healthy society

When families are strong, communities are strong. That naturally leads to a strong society. The definition of a " healthy" or "good" community often the subject of heated debate. Countless studies have explored the impacts of adoption, LGBTQ+ relationships, families with multiple ethnicities, and so on. Society is deeply invested in the strength of families because there's a domino effect. If families aren't doing well, a nation will suffer. If families are happy and healthy, the nation benefits.

I have examined my birth certificate many times, but the impact of a father not being listed now has so much more meaning. For every child with that same blank box, a part of their persona is missing also. I, like so many others, spend a lifetime trying to fill that void. It takes two people to produce a child; so it definitely takes more than two to provide every need. I end this neglectful case with a song, written by Whitney Houston called *The Greatest Love of All*. It was my class high school graduation song.

Suggested Therapies And Other Helpful Information:

National Alliance on Mental Illness:

Religion and spirituality are both rooted in trying to understand the meaning of life and, in some cases, how a relationship with a higher power may influence that meaning. While religion and spirituality are similar in foundation, they are very different in practice.

Religion is an organized, community-based system of beliefs, while spirituality resides within the individual and what they personally believe. "The idea of religion and spirituality is like a rectangle versus a square. Within religion there is spirituality, but if you have spirituality, it doesn't necessarily mean you have religion," says someone who practices both religion and spirituality.

Both religion and spirituality can have a positive impact on mental health. In some ways, they provide the same impact. For example: Both religion and spirituality can help a person tolerate stress by generating peace, purpose, and forgiveness. But benefits generally vary between the two due to their different nature.

Mental Health Benefits of Religion

Religion gives people something to believe in, provides a sense of structure, and typically offers a group of people to connect with over similar beliefs. These facets can have a large positive impact on mental health—research suggests that religiosity reduces suicide rates, alcoholism, and drug use. Here are some of religion's main mental health benefits.

Music Therapy: https://www.takingcharge.csh.umn.edu

Music therapy is the use of music to address the physical, emotional, cognitive, and social needs of a group or individual. It employs a variety of activities, such as listening to melodies, playing an instrument, drumming, writing songs, and guided imagery. Music therapy is appropriate for people of all ages, whether they are virtuosos or tone deaf, struggling with illnesses or totally healthy.

Music therapy touches all aspects of the mind, body, brain, and behavior. Music can provide a distraction for the mind, it can slow the rhythms of the body, and it can alter our mood, which in turn can influence behavior.

Trained and certified music therapists work in a variety of healthcare and educational settings. They often work with people suffering from emotional health issues such as grief, anxiety, and depression. They also help people address rehabilitative needs after a stroke, a traumatic head injury, or with chronic conditions like Parkinson's or Alzheimer's disease.

Music therapy sessions are designed with a number of factors in mind, including the clients' physical health, communication abilities, cognitive skills, emotional well-being, and interests. After weighing these factors along with the treatment goals, the therapist decides to employ either the creative or receptive process. (Note that you do not need to have musical abilities to benefit from either process. The music therapist will ensure that the activities address the needs and abilities of the client!)

In the creative process, the music therapist works with the client to actively create or produce the music. This may include composing a song, engaging in music or song improvisation, or drumming. In the receptive process, the therapist offers music listening experiences, such as using music to facilitate a client or group's relaxation. Clients or groups may then discuss thoughts, feelings, or ideas elicited by that music.

Music therapy sounds great (no pun intended). But does it work? The body of research surrounding music therapy continues to grow; check out the reports in the Journal of Music Therapy. You can also learn more about music therapy, including how to find a qualified therapist, by visiting the American Music Therapy Association.

Music therapy is the use of music to address the physical, emotional, cognitive, and social needs of a group or individual. It employs a variety of activities, such as listening to melodies, playing an instrument, drumming, writing songs, and guided imagery.

Somatic Therapy

How It Works

The theory behind somatic therapy is that the mind, body, spirit, and emotions are all related and connected to each other. As a result, the stress of past emotional and traumatic events affects the central nervous system and can cause changes in the body and even in body language, often resulting in altered facial expressions and posture as well as physical pain. Through developing awareness of the mind-body connection and using specific interventions, somatic therapy helps you to release the tension, anger, frustration, and other emotions that remain in your body from these past negative experiences. The goal is to help free you from the stress and pain that is preventing you from fully engaging in your life.

What to Look for in a Somatic Therapist

Somatic therapy can be integrated into other psychotherapy and counseling practices. Look for a licensed, experienced mental health professional with advanced, supervised training in somatic therapy techniques. In addition to finding someone with the appropriate educational background, experience, and positive approach, look for a therapist with whom you feel comfortable discussing personal issues.

Psilocybin therapy: https://Compasspathways.com

Psilocybin therapy is an approach being investigated for the treatment of mental health challenges. It combines the pharmacological effects of psilocybin, a psychoactive substance, with psychological support.

Psilocybin is an active ingredient in some species of mushrooms, often referred to as 'magic mushrooms'. We have developed a synthesized formulation of psilocybin, COMP 360, and are investigating the effectiveness of psilocybin therapy, initially in treatment-resistant depression.

Early studies conducted in pioneering academic centers have shown signals that psilocybin could be a safe and effective medicine for patients with depression, anxiety, addiction, and other mental illnesses, when administered with psychological support from specially trained therapists.

Why Learn to Meditate?

A selection of benefits that are associated with meditating.

While meditation isn't a cure-all, it can certainly provide some much-needed space in your life. Sometimes, that's all we need to make better choices for ourselves, our families, and our communities. And the most important tools you can bring with you to your meditation practice are a little patience, some kindness for yourself, and a comfortable place to sit.

When we meditate, we inject far-reaching and long-lasting benefits into our lives. And bonus: you don't need any extra gear or an expensive membership.

Here are five reasons to meditate:

Understanding your pain

Lower your stress

Connect better

Improve focus

Reduce brain chatter

Journaling:

The power of opening up People have been keeping diaries long before scientists thought to put them under microscopes. But in the past 30 years, hundreds of studies have uncovered the benefits of putting pen to paper with your deepest thoughts and feelings.

According to that research, journaling may help ease our distress when we're struggling. In a 2006 study, nearly 100 young adults were asked to spend 15 minutes journaling or drawing about a stressful event, or writing about their plans for the day, twice during one week. The people who journaled saw the biggest reduction in symptoms like depression, anxiety, and hostility, particularly if they were very distressed to begin with. This was true even though 80 percent had seldom journaled about their feelings and only 61 percent were comfortable doing so.

Why do we avoid journaling?

For one, it isn't always pleasant; I know that I sometimes have to force myself to sit down and do it. Cathartic is probably a better word. In fact, some research suggests that we can feel more anxious, sad, or guilty right after we write.

But in the long term, we can expect to cultivate a greater sense of meaning as well as better health. Various studies have found that people who do a bout of journaling have fewer doctor visits in the following half-year and reduced symptoms of chronic disease like asthma and arthritis.

Can your diary keep you healthy? Other research finds that writing specifically boosts our immune system, good news when the source of so much stress today is an infectious virus.

One older study even found that journaling could make vaccines more effective. In the experiment, some medical students wrote for four days in a row about their thoughts and feelings around some of the most traumatic experiences of their lives, from divorce to grief to abuse, while others simply wrote down their daily events and plans. Then, everyone received the Hepatitis B vaccine and two booster shots.

According to blood tests, the group who journaled about upsetting experiences had higher antibodies right before the last dose and two months later. While the other group had a perfectly healthy response to the vaccine, the authors write, journaling could make an important difference for people who are immune-compromised or for vaccines that don't stimulate the immune system as well.

"Expression of emotions concerning stressful or traumatic events can produce measurable effects on human immune responses," writes the University of Auckland's Keith J. Petrie and his colleagues.

Teletherapy:

Teletherapy is any remote therapy that uses technology to help the therapist and client communicate. Some examples of teletherapy include:

doing therapy sessions over the phone

having a group chat for group therapy

using video conferencing for individual, couples, or group therapy

receiving therapy via email or instant messenger

using apps that connect clients to therapists and offer therapy within the app

Benefits of teletherapy

Teletherapy provides a range of benefits in comparison with traditional therapy

Most research suggests that teletherapy can be as effective as in-person therapy. The benefits of seeking research-supported teletherapy with a licensed therapist include:

Greater access to a care trusted Source: Some people are unable to use traditional therapy due to physical disabilities, geographic location, or scheduling issues.

Lower costs: Teletherapy may help clients save money on treatment. Clients are also likely to incur fewer therapy-associated expenses when they do not have to travel to receive treatment or pay for childcare.

High satisfaction: Users of quality teletherapy report high satisfaction with treatment.

More privacy: People who choose teletherapy do not have to sit in busy waiting rooms but can seek treatment in the privacy of their own homes. For some, this alleviates privacy concerns.

Better public health: The COVID-19 health crisis demonstrates that the ability to seek medical care at home can slow the spread of illness and protect vulnerable populations. Teletherapy allows people to get mental health treatment at home without risking the spread of infection during epidemics and pandemics.

Some therapists may find that teletherapy suits their personal style and allows them to meet their practice goals. Some benefits include:

Reduced overheads: Maintaining an office can be expensive. Therapists who switch to a telehealth-only model can eliminate many of their overheads. Those who offer part-time teletherapy may be able to rent office space on just a few days of the week, lowering costs.

The ability to reach more clients: Telehealth may improve access to therapy, a trusted source for people with disabilities, financial worries, transportation difficulties, and other barriers. This improved access enables therapists to help more people. Widening their potential consumer base can help therapists earn more money.

Teletherapy is an ideal option for people who find it difficult to access therapy in person. It is also an excellent option for slowing the spread of illness, for example, during the COVID-19 pandemic or in the flu and cold season.

HOTLINE INFORMATION:

*Texas Abuse Hotline (800) 252-5200

* National Suicide Prevention Lifeline (800) 273-8255

If you or someone you know is in crisis—whether they are considering suicide or not—please call the toll-free Lifeline at 800-273-TALK (8255) to speak with a trained crisis counselor 24/7.

The National Suicide Prevention Lifeline connects you with a crisis center in the Lifeline network closest to your location. Your call will be answered by a trained crisis worker who will listen empathetically and without judgment. The crisis worker will work to ensure that you feel safe and help identify options and information about mental health services in your area. Your call is confidential and free.

Crisis Text Line – Text NAMI to 741-741

Connect with a trained crisis counselor to receive free, 24/7 crisis support via text message.

National Domestic Violence Hotline – Call 800-799-SAFE (7233)

Trained expert advocates are available 24/7 to provide confidential support to anyone experiencing domestic violence or seeking resources and information. Help is available in Spanish and other languages.

National Sexual Assault Hotline – Call 800-656-HOPE (4673)

Connect with a trained staff member from a sexual assault service provider in your area that offers access to a range of free services. Crisis chat support is available at Online Hotline. Free help, 24/7.

WORKS CITED

"Greatest Love of All" Video and Lyrics by Whitney Houston. https://www.onecommunityglobal.org/inspiring-popular-songs-greatest-love-of-all-by-whitney-houston-video-and-lyrics/

About psilocybin therapy :

Compass Pathways. https://compasspathways.com/our-research/psilocybin-therapy/about-psilocybin-therapy/

Commonly asked questions about child sexual abuse | CSA https://csaawarenessmonth.wordpress.com/2011/04/06/commonly-asked-questions-about-child-sexual-abuse/

DailyMed - ZIPRASIDONE- ziprasidone hydrochloride capsule. https://dailymed.nlm.nih.gov/dailymed/drugInfo.cfm?setid=72f4f662-b1e2-406f-8f5f-c3595c459a25

Fanapt. https://jeopardylabs.com/print/fanapt

How Journaling Can Help You in Hard Times. https://greatergood.berkeley.edu/article/item/how_journaling_can_help_you_in_hard_times

How to Meditate - Mindful. https://www.mindful.org/how-to-meditate/

NAMI HelpLine | NAMI: National Alliance on Mental Illness. https://nami.org/help

Nehemiah 8:10 NIV: Nehemiah said, " Go and enjoy choice https://biblehub.com/niv/nehemiah/8-10.htm

Somatic Therapy - Psychology Today. https://www.psychologytoday.com/us/therapy-types/somatic-therapy

Teletherapy: How it works - kazmobrain.com. https://kazmobrain.com/teletherapy-how-it-works/

Teletherapy: How it works - Medical News Today. https://www.medicalnewstoday.com/articles/teletherapy

Teletherapy: How it works - Medical News Today. https://www.medicalnewstoday.com/articles/teletherapy

The Big Apple: " We homeschool because we have seen the …. https://www.barrypopik.com/index.php/new_york_city/entry/we_homeschool_because/

The Importance of a Father in a Child's Life - Pediatric …. https://www.pediatricsoffranklin.com/resources-and-education/pediatric-care/the-importance-of-a-father-in-a-childs-life/

The Mental Health Benefits of Religion & Spirituality - NAMI. https://www.nami.org/Blogs/NAMI-Blog/December-2016/The-Mental-Health-Benefits-of-Religion-Spiritual

Voyeurism - Mental Health Disorders - Medicine.com. https://www.medicine.com/topic/voyeurism

Voyeuristic Disorder | Univadis. https://www.univadis.co.uk/viewarticle/voyeuristic-disorder-460143

What is music therapy? | Taking Charge of Your Health ....
https://www.takingcharge.csh.umn.edu/common-
questions/what-music-therapy

ABOUT THE AUTHOR

Artie was born in Bullard, Texas, in 1960. Against all odds, Artie graduated from Green B. Trimble Technical High School at seventeen, receiving the Grammar Award. She obtained her practical nursing license by eighteen from All Saints School of Vocational Nursing in Ft Worth, Texas, all while juggling single parenthood. Yes, Artie is genuinely the image of a strong black woman. For the past fifteen years, Artie has been a pediatric home health nurse. She recently started a small business making organic hair and body products. Momma Artie said her company name indeed fits her assertive personality.

Her passion for writing stemmed from the quick-thinking notes she used to communicate secretly with her mother during those horrifically abusive years, depicted in Got Me Ready. A riveting memoir of life from infancy. Her proudest accomplishments are her two children, six grandchildren, and one great-grand. Many more call her Momma or Granny.

Got Me Ready is her first book. It chronicles her strength and fortitude even as a small child. Artie single-handedly orchestrated her emancipation from cruelty, ensuring her chance at happiness. Quoting the great Maya Angelou, "There is no greater agony than bearing an untold story inside you."